Women at Work
in Australia
from the Gold Rushes
to World War II

Raelene Frances and Bruce Scates

CAMBRIDGE
UNIVERSITY PRESS

For our children, Bill and Alex

Published by the Press Syndicate of the University of Cambridge
The Pitt Building, Trumpington Street, Cambridge CB2 1RP, UK
40 West 20th Street, New York, NY 10011-4211, USA
10 Stamford Road, Oakleigh, Melbourne, Victoria 3166, Australia

© Cambridge University Press 1993
First published 1993

Printed in Hong Kong by Colorcraft

National Library of Australia cataloguing in publication data
Frances, Raelene.
Women at work in Australia from the gold rushes to World War II.
ISBN 0 521 38769 8.
1. Women — Employment — Australia — History. I. Scates, Bruce. II.
Title. (Series: Women in Australian History).
331.40994

Library of Congress cataloguing in publication data
Frances, Raelene.
Women at work in Australia: from the gold rushes to World War II
Raelene Frances and Bruce Scates.
— (Women in Australian history)
Summary: Examines the work undertaken by women in Australia
between the gold rushes of the 1850s and World War II.
ISBN 0 521 38769 8
1. Women — Employment — Australia — History — Juvenile literature.
[1. Women — Employment — Australia — History.] I. Scates, Bruce.
II. Title. III. Series.
HD6220.F73 1992
331.4'0994–dc20
92–14685
CIP
AC

A catalogue record for this book is available from the British Library.

ISBN 0 521 38769 8 paperback

Contents

Preface

In writing a book about urban women's work in the period between the 1850s gold rushes in the eastern colonies and World War II, we have tried to do two things. On the one hand we have outlined the changing patterns of women's employment, the kinds of work they did and the circumstances under which they did it. On the other we have attempted to convey a sense of the experience of work for the individual women concerned: what did their work mean to them, why were they compelled to do it and how did they respond when the nature of that work changed? The actual lives of actual women are the focus of this discussion. Chapter 1, for instance, presents a case study of Eleanor Lucas, tracing her life from poverty on the goldfields to the proprietorship of an innovative and important clothing firm.

In some ways Eleanor's life was exceptional—few women enjoyed such success. But in other ways it was not. In poverty and prosperity, Eleanor confronted the same sorts of dilemmas and opportunities faced by most women of her day. Her story is used to introduce the themes of the book as a whole. It shows how the contemporary ideal of women as dependent housewives and mothers was often different to the reality and it reminds us that their economic choices were not really choices at all. Rather, the nature of women's work was structured by a number of factors: ideological considerations of what work was thought to be suited to a woman; economic considerations of what the market required; the needs and contribution of the family; and the training and initiative of the individual woman as well. All women negotiated these structures as their personalities and backgrounds best allowed.

Until about fifteen years ago the life and work of such women was peripheral to historical concerns. Since then academic and non-academic historians have endeavoured to enlarge the scope of history, alerting us to the importance of women's role. But rewriting Australian history is not simply a matter of adding women to the history that went before. The challenge is not just to include women, but to change the agenda of history as a whole. As such we are interested in the home as well as the workplace, the family as well as the community, the private as well as the public sphere. This book is in keeping with the concerns of social history; it is a history about people as well as politics, a history written from below.

It is a people's history in more ways than one. Throughout this book we invite readers to take history into their own hands. Visiting a workplace or conducting an oral history is not just a way of recreating the past. It also shifts the focus of learning away from an individual textbook towards the community. Moreover, we have invited our readers to make their own judgments. While the narrative of this book offers a challenging reassessment of women's life and work, its extensive documents, written and visual, raise questions all of their own. This book is part of the effort to retrieve women's voice in history, a voice historians are only just beginning to respect and understand.

Acknowledgments

Like most books, this one has incurred a number of debts. We wish to thank the many unions, businesses and private agencies who granted us access to their records and the archivists and librarians who assisted us in our work. Special thanks are due to Mandy Bede, Mimi Colligan, Robyn Faulkner, Kandy-Jane Henderson and Joanna Sassoon for their help in acquiring material from Melbourne and Perth.

While much of this book was based on research for our doctoral and MA theses, additional research was made possible by Christine Wood of Auckland University's inter-library loan section and the staff of the Parliamentary Library in Wellington. Thanks are also due to Pam Goode, Ian Grant, Denise Hill and the staff of Auckland University Creche for child-care; to Auckland University Research Committee for funding; to Annette Hallal and Gary Underwood of Cambridge University Press and Sue Harvey, our editor, for advice and encouragement and a healthy measure of trust.

Finally we are indebted to Kay Daniels, the series editor, and to Barbara Batt who typed and retyped a complex and ever-expanding manuscript.

Rae Frances
Bruce Scates

1   Introduction

Eleanor Hargreaves was just three years old when she arrived in Victoria in 1852. Her family was one of the thousands who made their way to the diggings, leaving the settled life of Yorkshire in the hope of striking gold in Ballarat. But for Eleanor's family, as for many others, immigration was a gamble which never paid off. Mrs Hargreaves died a few years after their arrival in the colony, her health apparently broken by hardship and disappointment. Eleanor and her brother were cared for by friends and neighbours, leaving the father free to scratch a living from the soil.

At the age of fourteen Eleanor too joined the work-force. Two years of indifferent schooling had taught her the basics of writing and arithmetic—all the education necessary to tend the houses of the rich. After four years 'in service' she left to marry a carrier, John Price. She was eighteen, small in frame but keen, resolute and strong in body and mind.

Eleanor soon found she had exchanged one form of service for another. For the next twelve years she produced a child at two-year intervals. Three daughters and two sons survived infancy. Later deaths were both emotionally traumatic and economically costly. Eleanor's eldest son died in 1878, when he had just reached the age to bring home a wage. The same year her husband was killed in an industrial accident. She was left to provide for four children, the youngest of whom was a seven-month-old baby. Eleanor was thirty-one and penniless.

For a time charity helped out. A public appeal raised enough to keep her family in food, clothing and shelter. More importantly it provided the means of earning a livelihood: a sewing machine.

From 1878 to 1886, Eleanor and her treadle machine toiled well into the night. Supplied with cloth from a nearby draper's shop, she turned out shirts and underwear. She was paid by the piece, and her average daily earnings brought in just enough to survive. In 1886 there was a brief respite to her hardship: Eleanor married William Lucas, a widowed miner, and went to live on his farm

A determined and successful woman: Eleanor Lucas, nee Hargreaves, in middle age, circa 1900.

(M. White, *The Golden Thread*, Melbourne, E. Lucas & Co. Pty Ltd, 1963)

outside Ballarat. Two years later a mining accident claimed her second husband. She was once again 'on her own'.

This time Eleanor was better placed to survive. Her children had grown, so the family home could become a workshop which could produce four times as much 'whitework' as before. The business now had the scope to diversify. After her husband's death, Eleanor worked as a machinist for a Ballarat tailoring firm then returned to working from home. She passed her newly found skills on to her eldest daughter. Another daughter, aged fourteen, was sent out to work for a nearby tailor and quickly learnt the art of cutting clothes. The youngest daughter, barely twelve, was set to service the family's labours, carrying material and clothing to and from the draper's shop and pressing the finished garments. By the 1880s the frontier town of Ballarat had grown to a large provincial city and Eleanor's industry was well rewarded. Her shirts and underwear found a ready market; an underclothing manufacturer was as much a contributor to economic growth as factories and farms. Most importantly, Eleanor possessed the prerequisite of every successful business: capital for investment. The sale of her husband's farm earnt enough to extend the family cottage. A workshop was built on to the existing dwelling, machines installed and benches constructed. By the 1890s, Eleanor's 'Busy Bee' Factory employed sixteen girls beside her own daughters. All laboured, as she once had, for a few shillings a week.

The first purpose-built premises of E. Lucas & Co.—the 'Busy Bee' Factory, Ballarat, 1894. Eleanor Lucas is visible standing with her son and daughters behind the staff of predominantly teenage girls.

(M. White, *The Golden Thread*, Melbourne, E. Lucas & Co. Pty Ltd, 1963, p. 11)

The twentieth century saw the consolidation of Eleanor's labours. Her modest workroom in James Street gave way to a factory and showroom in the centre of the city which employed over four hundred workers on three hundred high-speed machines. The organisation of work was also changing. Gone were the days when Eleanor would piece together an entire garment, working at a pace that suited her temperament and mood. By the late 1890s each of the 'Lucas girls' (Eleanor had taken the name of her second husband) attended to a small part of the production process: sewing buttonholes, cutting cloth or pressing garments. At this time Eleanor herself drifted away from the business she had founded. Her son became a partner in the firm in 1898 and assumed most of the practical responsibilities of management. Eleanor's daughters, by contrast, left the firm to establish families of their own. Marriage was to mark the end of their careers outside the home.

Women still had a large part to play in the firm. Edward Price (Eleanor's son by her first husband) relied on the unpaid assistance of his wife, Elvira, and the hired help of saleswomen and overseers. Over 80 per cent of the firm's employees were women well below the age of eighteen. However, control of the firm passed increasingly into the hands of men. By the beginning of World War II, the intimate family business had been replaced by a modern factory. Men ran the firm from glass-walled offices on the second floor, while women toiled below. The firm of E. Lucas and Co. Pty Ltd honoured Eleanor only in name.

Eleanor's story is by no means exceptional. Australia's history is littered with examples of women rising above adversity, carving out a living for themselves and their families. Some, like Eleanor, achieved a measure of success and recognition. But most have been forgotten, their crucial contribution to an industry or a family acknowledged only by those who worked beside them. The purpose of this book is to redress this imbalance in the historical memory, retrieving something of the ordinary yet extraordinary lives of women.

Eleanor's story is of particular interest because it covers many of the themes central to this book. Like all the women whose lives are examined here, Eleanor was a provider, her labour sustaining not just herself but also her family. Contrary to the expectations of her era, Eleanor was not supported by her husband. Much of her time was spent in the work-force, struggling to balance her paid labour with unpaid domestic responsibilities. Indeed, it was often women who brought home the wage. The Victorian census of 1891 noted that about one-fifth of 'breadwinners' were female. The real figure was probably even higher.

(See Documents 1.1 and 1.2.)

Many female breadwinners had lost their husbands in industrial accidents. Work in the nineteenth century was difficult and hazardous. Men were drowned at sea and crushed by machinery; their blood was poisoned with toxic chemicals; their backs were broken in falls from scaffolding. Eleanor's first

DOCUMENT 1.1

'Bachelors' and 'spinsters'

**Percentage never married in selected age groups
Victoria, 1881–1901**

	Males			Females		
Year	20–24	25–29	45–49	20–24	25–29	45–49
1881	87.9	57.2	19.5	67.9	33.0	4.5
1891	89.5	60.5	19.1	69.3	38.3	7.4
1901	91.6	66.1	19.0	77.8	50.8	12.9

(Adapted from P. McDonald, *Marriage in Australia: Age at First Marriage and Proportions Marrying, 1860–1871*, ANU Press, Canberra, 1974, pp. 112, 134)

• How might these statistics be relevant to a study of women's work?

husband was crushed beneath the wheels of his lorry; her second buried beneath the rubble of a mine shaft. In some cases entire communities made do without their menfolk. The Bulli coalmine collapse in 1887 claimed the lives of eighty-one workers: they left behind them thirty-seven widows, 120 children and a large number of unborn babies.

(See Document 1.3.)

DOCUMENT 1.2

Women in the work-force

Female work-force participation rates by age, all females, Victoria, 1891

(Victorian Census, 1891)

• • • •

As to the number that leave the trade to get married that is only a bogey; because there are not such a great number leave our factories to get married; and not only that, a large proportion when they do get married come back; some through their husbands being out of work, some through unfortunate marriages, and some through being left widows with large families . . .

(Evidence of Mrs Sarah Muir, Shops and Factories Royal Commission, Victoria, 1901, p. 436)

• Does the graph above seem to support or contradict Sarah Muir's statements?

DOCUMENT 1.3

Insure against accidents

(*Boomerang*, 13 December 1890)

● What does this document tell us about the hazards of everyday life in colonial Australia?
● Which 'market' does the document appeal to? Why?

A dead husband was bad enough, but a sick one was a double burden. Many women had to work to support injured, aged or ailing husbands who were unable to work and possibly in need of expensive medical treatment. Some women had to work to supplement their husbands' wages, which were often too small to support their families. Work in Eleanor's time was seasonal and intermittent; long bouts of unemployment or underemployment occurred between jobs and men were often obliged to seek work

(Mr Justice Higgins, reporting on findings in 1909 dispute between miners and Broken Hill Proprietary Company Ltd, Commonwealth Arbitration Reports, Vol. 3, p. 26)

• How appropriate are the descriptions 'breadwinner' and 'dependant' for the husband and wife in the family?

DOCUMENT 1.4

'Breadwinners' and 'dependants'

One labourer, with 8/7½ per day, expends—or rather his wife expends—£2/18/9 per week—7/0 more than his receipts . . . I ascertained the pathetic fact that, in many cases, including the case just mentioned, the wife adds to the little income by laundry work or nursing, or by taking in lodgers . . . The fact that the mother of the household is so often found leaving her home, even her young children for a day's work, is significant.

far from home. If their husbands were out of work, absent or had deserted, women had to support entire families. These were the starving times, times of want and despair.

(See Document 1.4.)

A woman's ability to provide for her family depended on a number of factors. The most obvious, in Eleanor's case, was the life cycle of the family itself. The first years were usually the hardest. Unable to leave their young children, women like Eleanor were forced to labour in their own homes. 'Outwork', as it was known, had many advantages for employers. Putting work out to women like Eleanor was cheaper than maintaining an expensive factory; it was also more efficient. Eleanor was paid by the piece; economic necessity drove her harder than the most watchful of employers.

The outworker was an isolated worker. Thousands of 'Eleanors' toiled in their homes, unable to discuss their common grievances or band together in pursuit of better wages and conditions. Indeed, such women competed with one another, desperate to keep whatever work they could find. In a sense, then, this was a captive work-force. Chained to the home by their children and other dependants, women accepted work on their employers' terms. The employers' terms were never very favourable. The earnings of an outworker varied from individual to individual, but they were always well below those of factory workers. Outwork was also known as 'sweating'. Women like Eleanor toiled well into the night in the hope of earning enough to live. An eighteen-hour day was not uncommon.

As their young children grew the options open to women widened. With her youngest child at school, Eleanor was able to seek work further afield, improving her skills in the process. Equally importantly, changes in the life cycle of her family had made an asset of a liability. With Eleanor's children old enough to work, they could contribute to the family economy. But the life cycles of families are never stable or predictable. Another pregnancy could drag a family back into poverty, as could illness or unemployment among any of its adult members. Eleanor was lucky in being able to marshal the resources of her family with astounding ability.

(See Document 1.5.)

Eleanor's 'luck' was not confined to her own family. Women worked within a wider economic context, the successes of their business or the well-being of their families being dependent on fickle market forces. Eleanor was fortunate enough to begin her business in a period of economic upturn: she was able to sell her husband's land at a speculatively inflated price, secure money for reinvestment and find a ready market for her clothing in a growing urban population. Had Eleanor's husband died at the beginning of the 1890s depression the story might well have been different. As it was the Busy Bee Factory actually benefited from the depression. With their husbands and fathers unemployed, the 'Lucas girls' were prepared to work for whatever wage Eleanor Lucas cared to offer. The firm could continue to function because it was an essential industry—even in a depression people could not endure Ballarat's winter without decent underwear. There was a commonly-held belief that women took men's jobs in times of economic recession. However, the 'girls' at the Lucas factory continued to work because their labour was needed; the labour of their fathers (employed principally in housing, furnishing and manufacturing) was not. In both the 1890s and the 1930s depressions women's unemployment was slightly lower than that of men's—but the gender division of labour remained largely unaltered.

'The sweated outworker' by Lionel Lindsay. By the time this sketch appeared, outwork was less readily available due to the increase in factory production of clothing in the first decade of the twentieth century.

(*Lone Hand*, March 1911)

DOCUMENT 1.5

Report on sweating

. . . though difficult to understand, it is certainly true, that many females prefer working at home, even when the prices obtained are lower. It must be remembered that by working at home a woman has no limit to the number of hours she may work; she has also the opportunity of help from her mother (who could not leave home to go into the factory), and younger sisters (who are too young to be allowed to go to work); so that, although she may have worked considerably more than 48 hours in the week, she may, on the other hand, have been able to take a holiday, and at the same time be able to show as much money earned as if she had been going to the factory regularly, and had to conform to rules, etc., which are oftentimes irksome to her. It is also probable that a man employing only a few girls can get work done cheaper than in a large factory, because he allows the girls more liberty; they stop away from work when they like, and when they return nothing is said to them'.

(Report of Chief Inspector of Factories, Victoria, 1889)

● We have seen some reasons why women did outwork. What other reasons does this report give us for the reluctance of girls to work in factories?

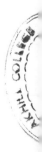

Woman's Rights.

(FOR THE BULLETIN.)

It is Woman's Right to scrub,
And to cook our daily "grub,"
But it's not her right to search us when we come
home from the Club.

It is her right our bread to bake
And to fry our chop and steak,
But it's not her right to think we should keep
sober for her sake.

It is Woman's Right to say
Just what *we* think, and she may
Do that, but musn't think of hitting out in her
own way.

It is her right to dust and sweep,
And the house in order keep,
But it's not her right to buy up things because she
thinks they're cheap.

It is not her place to think,
And it's not her right to drink,
Nor to ever want to visit a theatre or a rink.

It is Woman's Right to know
What will please her master, so
She can bring the very liquor that will drive away
his woe.

It is Woman's Right, you see,
To do many things, but she
Mustn't trespass on the province of the Everlasting
He.
                                         E. DEMPSEY.

The division of labour by gender was a social construction which determined where women could work as much as did personal ability or market forces. An understanding of this division of labour is central to an understanding of Eleanor's chequered career (or indeed the working lives of any of the women studied in this book). Entering the clothing trade was in fact an extension of Eleanor's earlier role as a wife and mother: once she darned socks and fashioned garments for her family; now she sold the same services to others. As Eleanor's business grew, the gender division of work manifested itself in a number of ways. Mindful that the role of manager and entrepreneur were not always considered feminine, Eleanor took on the role of mother of her work-force. The 'Lucas girls', as they were known, were watched over by a matriarch; cloth was cut and measured with all the economy of a housewife. As the responsibilities of management became too onerous, Eleanor passed on the position to her son rather than her daughters. Sons were thought to be temperamentally suited to the world of trade and finance and daughters destined to marry and raise children.

(See Document 1.6.)

The strength of this gender ideology influenced the work of every woman in every occupation. On the one hand, it defined the industries in which women could work; the building trade, for instance, was considered no place for a lady. But it also limited the jobs a woman could do within a particular industry. Eleanor's trade is one such example: women in the clothing trade were permitted to sew cloth and cut whitework but not to design a man's suit. That, as one tailor explained, required a 'masculine' mystique. Moreover, the sexual division of labour served to marginalise women within the work-force. Because their real roles were seen as those of wives and mothers, their paid labour was devalued. With few exceptions, a woman could not have a career—her time at work was constantly interrupted by children and chores. The result was that women were confined to casual, low-paid and 'unskilled' sections of the work-force: these were supposedly the jobs a woman did best.

(See Document 1.7.)

Whatever job a woman took, her choice was seldom a free one. As Eleanor's story shows, a woman's options were limited through circumstance; the needs of her family mattered more than personal ability, and definitions of what work was acceptable for a woman were as significant as the economic climate of the day. This tension between choice and necessity, expectation and reality is a recurrent theme in this book. Such was the pattern of women's lives of labour.

This sarcastic poem on the position of women in the colonial gender order appeared at a time when women were campaigning to obtain greater control over their lives.
(*Bulletin*, 20 December 1890, p. 23)

DOCUMENT 1.6

The sex of labour

It is dangerous to teach a girl that 'woman is man's equal in everything'. It will inevitably result in a desire to adopt a man's career as much more exciting than cooking dinners and nursing babies. The 'economic independence of women' must result in the abolition of family life, as the mother of young children cannot be economically independent.

• • • •

('A socialist Sunday School', *Liberty and Progress*, 25 September 1906, p. 135)

Nature fashioned and destined man to be a breadwinner. He has no other raison d'être. Unless he works as a breadwinner there is nothing whatever for him to do, and the inevitable penalty of masculine idleness is degeneration. On the other hand, Nature fashioned and destined woman to be a mother. Nature lavished all the resources of her genius in equipping woman with creative functions, and she decreed that those creative functions (and their derivative and subject faculties) should be adequately exercised under penalty of blasted health and a shattered nervous system. When a man works he does what Nature commands, and the only thing that he can do. When a woman works (as a breadwinner, of course), she has to put aside the things that she can do best, and the only things she ought to be concerned with, and in defiance of Nature she undertakes the things which she was never intended to perform, and for the performance of which she is least qualified. The displacement of male workers by female breadwinners inexorably resolves itself into a racial issue. It threatens man with moral and physical degradation. It threatens woman with disease and decay. But, above all, it menaces the rising generation, for what sort of children can we hope will spring from the union of idle and degenerate males with females who have run counter to Nature during the most critical years of their life, and have thereby disordered their creative functions, as all women must do who for the sake of money and an illusory independence disobey Nature's most fundamental law?

• • • •

('The sex of labour', *Age*, 12 September 1911)

● What do these writers see as woman's 'proper sphere'? Why? Do you agree with them?

In Australia, also, although to a smaller degree, there has been increased employment and higher wages for women. It is to be hoped that this will continue. A great deal of nonsense has been talked and written on this subject. The very people who hold up their hands in horror because women do light work in factories and machine shops, look on unperturbed while seeing them do the far harder work of washing clothes and scrubbing floors. In our opinion much of the work now done by men, clerical work for example, ought to be done by women, while much of the work done by women ought to be done by men.

('The Employment of Women', *Australasian Manufacturer*, 25 September 1920, p. 17)

● Compare the attitudes expressed here with those from the *Age* and *Liberty and Progress* above. Can you think of any reasons why the points of view are so different?

DOCUMENT 1.7

Changing distribution of women in the work-force

Percentage of women in employment at the Census

	1901	1911	1921	1933
Primary production				
Agriculture, pastoral, dairying	6.04	4.09	2.17	3.37
Other	0.02	0.02	0.09	0.06
Total	6.06	4.11	2.26	3.43
Manufacturing and construction				
of articles	20.24	22.74	17.12	13.15
Other	3.14	5.68	9.19	10.49
Total	23.38	28.42	26.31	23.64
Transport and communication				
Transport	0.35	0.38	0.62	0.78
Communicaton	0.69	0.87	0.96	1.23
Total	1.04	1.25	1.58	2.01
Commerce and finance				
Property and finance	1.90	1.91	1.38	1.85
Commerce	8.14	10.66	14.44	17.42
Total	10.04	12.57	15.82	19.27
Public authority and professional				
Health	3.54	4.37	5.81	6.13
Education	7.20	6.84	7.79	6.16
Others	2.04	2.43	4.83	6.08
Total	12.78	13.64	18.43	18.37
Entertainment, sport and recreation	0.28	0.33	0.51	0.68
Personal and domestic service				
Private domestic service	30.61	26.80	21.42	21.39
Hotels, boarding houses and restaurants	12.12	10.17	11.37	8.23
Others	3.69	2.71	2.30	2.98
Total	46.42	39.68	35.09	32.60

(Commonwealth of Australia Census, 1901–1933)

• This table shows the changing distribution of women in the work-force from 1901 to 1933 expressed as percentages of the total female work-force at any given time. What does it reveal about the changing pattern of female employment between 1901 and 1933?

Notes

Eleanor Lucas—The case study of Eleanor Lucas is based on a company history: Mollie White, *The Golden Thread*, E. Lucas & Co., Ballarat, 1963, and other documentary sources.

SUGGESTIONS FOR STUDY

For discussion

1 If Eleanor's first husband had died in the 1970s rather than the 1870s, how and why would her options have been different?

2 Do children of today contribute as much to their families' economic survival as Eleanor's children did?

3 In the nineteenth century, the average marriage lasted less than ten years. Do you think marriages last longer now? Are the reasons for this the same today as in Eleanor's day?

4 What is 'gender ideology'? How does it affect the kinds of work women and men do?

5 How does the 'family life cycle' affect a woman's ability to undertake paid work?

6 What is outwork? Why does it prevail to this day?

To write about

1 The gender or sexual division of labour refers to the phenomenon whereby women and men do different sorts of work. Make three lists, showing which kinds of work were done in the nineteenth century by men, women, and both sexes.

2 Imagine you are Eleanor Lucas. Write a letter to a friend in England describing your life and aspirations in 1868.

3 Write another letter to the same friend, but this time date it 1889.

4 Pretend you are a sewing machine retailer. Write an advertising brochure to persuade women to buy your product. (Note: You are able to sell these machines on time-payment.)

5 It was not uncommon for two or even three generations of women to work in the same factory. Compare the experience of a grandmother and granddaughter employed by the Lucas clothing firm. How did the nature of work and the relationship between employer and employee change over time?

Community resources

The family

1 Compile a family tree. Include the occupations of all your female forebears, the names and birthplaces of their children and estimate the time they spent in and out of the paid work-force. Is there any evidence of upward or downward social mobility? Much of this information may be recorded in family bibles and memorabilia. The rest you can find out by interviewing relatives and their friends.

2 Interview (if possible) your mother and grandmother. Prepare case histories of their working lives. What experiences do they have in common? How did their respective life choices change over time?

3 Rummage through the family garage, attic or garden. Can you find any artefacts which have a bearing on women's working lives?

4 Do any of the elderly members of your family live in nursing homes? Visit them and prepare case histories of them and their friends.

5 Collect all the family birth certificates you can find. Are the occupations of the mothers recorded? What other information might be of use to historians? Why?

2 Domestic Service

'Live-in' service

Not all working-class women were as successful as Eleanor Lucas. Most toiled throughout their lives in homes, shops and factories, earning barely enough to live. Many, like Eleanor, began their working lives as domestic servants.

For most of the nineteenth century, domestic service was the principal employer of women's labour. In 1891, for instance, it accounted for over 40 per cent of the paid female work-force. Service itself was divided into a myriad of occupations. Mindful that the number of servants one could employ was a measure of social status, wealthy families like the Parkes of Sydney boasted the services of a seamstress, a housemaid, a lady's maid, a laundress, a dairy maid, a nursemaid and a cook. Less affluent families made do with less. Living in North Fitzroy in the late 1880s, Reynold Johns and family relied on a single servant, principally employed as a cook. Florrie Robinson's work was made easier by the help of the Johns children. Even the daughters of a well-paid civil servant were required to learn the arts of cooking and cleaning, if only in preparation for the day they would manage households of their own. The needs of the Johns family, and other similar families, changed over the years. A nursemaid was indispensable for any middle-class mother keen to keep her place in 'society'; in later years the nursery would be converted to a bedroom and a lady's maid employed in her place.

The needs of employers changed but not as quickly as domestic servants changed their employers. Domestic servants were always in short supply and (indentures and contracts notwithstanding) they moved frequently from one situation to another. The fluidity of the profession meant that a young woman stood some chance of improving (if only slightly) her wages, status and conditions. Eleanor, for instance, probably began her career as a kitchenhand, the least skilled and lowest rung of the 'trade'. By careful observation and experimenting on her 'employer's digestion', she might well have become a cook and sought a better situation. Others graduated from nursemaid to lady's maid or worked their way up from the laundry to the kitchen.

But progress in the trade was not very well rewarded. A live-in cook earnt fifteen shillings a week in 1882, along with her keep. The laundress and housemaid who toiled alongside her did so for a few shillings less. In each case, their hours were long and unpredictable. Generally a maid worked from seven in the morning to ten at night, snatching her meals in between cooking, serving or cleaning up those of her employer. No time was her own; once one chore was done another was always waiting and she was always on call to attend the household's every need. In all but the sternest of families, Sunday morning was considered a holiday. Some holiday! Domestic servants accompanied their employers to church and sat several pews behind them. Then they washed and pressed their own clothing and, if time was left, wrote to their families. The work was as hard as it was unrelenting. In the days before automatic washing machines, clothing was scrubbed, boiled, raised up to drain, wrung and hung out on clothes lines. Much of this labour took place in the laundry, usually a small and badly ventilated building separate from the house, and intolerably hot. In temperatures of well over 38°C, women dragged clothing from boiling water and wrenched it, steaming and dripping, through their wringers. With this and every subsequent wringing they lifted loads heavier than a sack of potatoes and far less manageable. Even then the work was not over. After being hung out and dried, clothing was pressed with a heavy iron, stacked and folded. All this required skill, strength and dexterity; burnt linen or crumpled frills were enough to enrage most employers. (See Document 2.1.)

Work inside the colonial household was equally difficult. Dust gathered on rugs and sheltered in curtains, spread a thick film across picture frames and ornaments and dulled the gloss of highly polished tables. Every morning, sneezing servants would drag carpets or curtains outside, beat them, and drag them back; wipe and carefully reposition a hundred fragile heirlooms; and wipe over all the ornate woodwork in the house. By late morning the dust would once again have settled, awaiting the white finger of the 'mistress' on her tour of inspection. Cooking was no less demanding than cleaning. From one season to another wood-fire stoves were closely tended; the slightest fluctuation in temperature could spell the ruin of dinner. Employers' tastes were equally fickle. One week the cook could be abused for unsavoury or monotonous fare, and the next for her extravagance. Without the aid of refrigerators or microwaves, leftovers were to be recycled in as economic and appetising a way as possible. One mistress even measured the pudding sent back to the kitchen, fearful lest cook help herself to tomorrow's dinner.

The cook may well have been hungry. Board and lodgings were provided by employers so it was in their interests to maintain the work-force as cheaply as possible. As late as the 1920s, 'girls' who served their employers all kinds of delicacies subsisted on a diet of bread and honey. Even the tea they drank was rationed, and like all things they consumed, of inferior quality. Lodgings were

DOCUMENT 2.1

The hollow maiden

A Parlourmaid
'I want a parlourmaid.'
        'Well, let me see
If you were God, what kind of maid she'd be.'

'She would be tall,
She would be fair,
She would have slender limbs,
A delicate air;
And yet for all her beauty
She would walk
Among my guests unseen
And through their talk
Her voice would be the sweet voice of a bird,
Not listened to, though heard.'

'And now I know the girl you have in mind
Tell me her duties, if you'd be so kind.'

'Why, yes!
She must know names of wines
And never taste them—
Must handle fragile cups
And never break them—

Must fill my rooms with flowers
And never wear them—

Must serve my daughter's secrets
And not share them.'

'Madam, you are no God, that's plain to see.
I'll just repeat what you have said to me.

You say your maid must look in Helen fashion
Golden and white
And yet her loveliness inspire no passion,
Give no delight.

Your intimate goods of home must owe their
    beauty
To this girl's care
But she'll not overstep her path of duty
Nor seek to share

Through loving or enjoying or possessing
The least of them.
        Why, she's not human, by your own
    confessing,
And you condemn

Your rational self in every word you're speaking!
Please understand
You'll find the hollow maiden you are seeking
In fairyland.'

not much better. In mansions of twenty rooms, the staff slept in small quarters adjoining kitchens or laundries. A generous employer might provide a basin to wash in, but generally the servants bathed in troughs in the laundry. They ate in the kitchen, usually among the pots and pans. Uniforms were not provided by their employers, and maids scraped together what money they could to buy, make or repair them.

(See Document 2.2.)

Poor pay, long hours and hard work were the least of the servants' worries. Most intolerable of all were the relationships between servants and their 'superiors'. In the nineteenth century, servants were considered a caste separate and distinct from that of their employers. They were isolated from the families they

(D. Modjeska and M. Pizer (eds), *The Poems of Lesbia Harford*, Angus & Robertson, Sydney, 1985, pp.110–11)

• Employers' expectations of their servants were not always reasonable. Lesbia Harford, poet, feminist and labour activist, wrote this piece in the early twenties. Why does she describe the 'ideal' parlourmaid as 'a hollow maiden'?

DOCUMENT 2.2

The domestic's grievance

DOMESTIC SERVANTS.

TO THE EDITOR OF THE HERALD.

Sir.— Will you allow me space in your paper to refer to the way poor domestic servants are treated. People talk about the long hours of shop girls, who go to business from 9 till 6, except Saturdays; but the domestic is expected to rise at 6 in the morning, and retire at 10. Although we are not really kept at work all that time, we cannot feel that we have done, as where dinner is at 7 we cannot finish washing up till half-past 8 or a quarter to 9; and after that there is tea or supper to get of some kind, and then trot upstairs with hot water to the bedrooms. I know some who by that time feel completely tired out. Where is the real rest to come in? There is none on the Sabbath. We are supposed to have one evening a week out. By a great effort we manage to get away by half-past 7. We are by many employers expected to be in by 10 — a thing impossible under some circumstances. I am cook and laundress, and am expected to do the washing, while no other of my duties must be neglected in consequence. I have to prepare a hot lunch, also a dinner of soup, fish, entrées joints, and sweets, stand over a hot stove all day through the week, and on Sunday, instead of finding less to do, as we all expect from Christian people who go to church and repeat the Commandment, "Remember the Sabbath day to keep it holy. Six days shalt thou labour and do all that thou hast to do, and rest on the seventh," we find that our employers make a point of asking friends to dinner, and often have callers to afternoon tea. We know they have time and opportunity all the week. I have lived in a Jewish family, and have found far more consideration on our Sabbath Day from them than from members of the Church of England. A few of us feel that we should like to organise a servants' union. There are many good servants ready and willing to support it. We would have rules which would prevent our being imposed upon without doing anything which would inconvenience the ladies. We find that is the reason why many good girls go to almost any kind of business so that they may get Sunday and some evenings free. I have heard them say they would prefer being domestic servants were it not for the bondage.

I am, &c,   A DOMESTIC.

(*Sydney Morning Herald*, 11 August 1890)

● What does 'A Domestic' tell us about her hours of labour? Why were Sundays and evenings considered times a girl should call her own?

lived with, servicing their every need but denied physical comforts and intimacies. Not only was the work itself demeaning; servants were required to address the employers as 'sir' or 'madam', wear ridiculous frocks and caps, cringe and curtsy. For their part, employers assumed the authority (but few of the responsibilities) of de facto parents. Young women were forbidden to see men who might pose a moral danger, their leisure time was monitored and their work supervised by ill-qualified or unreasonable employers. Nor were their masters always the kind of folk to inspire respect or obedience. In the fluid social structure of Eleanor's youth it was not unknown for a girl to begin in service, marry well and herself become a mistress.

More usually employers were the *nouveau riche*; a class which had made its fortune on wool or gold and learnt none of the responsibilities which ideally attended established wealth. Whether or not a family was establishment, sexual transgressions were commonplace. Servant 'girls' were sometimes harassed or even raped by unscrupulous masters. Often they made easy victims: who would complain to a mistress and place at stake her job and reputation? This is not to suggest that domestic servants were completely powerless. A good cook had many advantages over a poor one; a careful lady's maid sometimes won her mistress's affection and trust. But whatever concessions a girl might win, the relationship between master and servant was never an equal one. With a change of mood or circumstance, the best of servants could fall from favour: all were potential victims of their masters' arbitrary rule.

(See Document 2.3.)

Rule and rebellion often went together. Australian-born servants were generally considered the hardest to handle: the

THE SIGN-LANGUAGE.

EUROPEAN LADY (to newly-engaged housemaid): "WHEN I WAVE MY HAND YOU HAVE TO COME."

COLONIAL GIRL: "YES, MUM, AND WHEN I SHAKE MY HEAD, THEN I WON'T COME."

Cartoons such as this were common in late nineteenth-century Australia. What does it say about the balance of power between mistress and servant?

(*Bulletin*, 8 November 1890, p. 14)

DOCUMENT 2.3

As good as her master?

4304.   Do the domestics suffer grievances as well as the needlewomen? — Yes, very much so; and that is why the public cannot get servants. I would not recommend any girl to go.
4305.   It is insufficient food? — Yes; in some places.
4306.   And bad accommodation? — Yes; and the food is all locked away except at certain hours. Then they have no time for recreation except one Sunday every fortnight and one evening after 8 o'clock.
4307.   Do you think it is a general thing for a considerable number of domestics to be allowed out only one evening a week? — Yes; the majority.
4308.   Not allowed out in the daytime at all? — No; except to run messages.
4309.   As regards the majority who are not allowed out in the daytime, would it not be inconvenient for them, in the matter of buying their goods, if they were prohibited from doing it after 6 o'clock? — I believe the rule is that they get a day off every month.
4310.   But for this they are only allowed out after tea, and would it not be inconvenient for them not to be able to buy after 6 o-clock? — No; because they could arrange to buy at another time.
4311.   They would arrange to go out in the daytime? — Yes; or leave it till the day they are off.

Mrs A.A.Milne   4312.   Can women always think what they want a month ahead? — Yes, pretty well;
April 28th 1892   but there would be no mistress bad enough not to allow her girl to go out for half an hour to do shopping.
4313.   Then you think this ill-treatment is the reason why so many girls are disinclined to go into domestic service? — It is one cause.
4314.   Are there others? — One great reason is that as South Australians we are thoroughly British, and the poor people love their children as much as the rich love theirs, and they like to have them round the fire-side as much as possible. To use a common phrase, Jack is as good as his master.

(Evidence of Mrs Agnes Milne, Shops and Factories Royal Commission, South Australia, 1892)

• Why, in Mrs Milne's opinion, were women 'disinclined to go into domestic service'?

rough life of the colonies did little to teach them their 'proper station'. Irish girls were considered equally unreliable. Matrons assigned to the voyage classified the girls by background and disposition. A 'placid lass' with a good hand at sewing would find a place in the best of Sydney's households; a 'strong-willed girl' or one of 'lazy habits' would be sent at once to the country where she could expect the harshest of employers. But breaking a servant's will was harder than master or mistress imagined. Employers frequently complained of their servants' reluctance to work. Many, like visiting Englishman, R. E. N. Twopenny, attributed this to the stupidity of their class and race.

Unfortunately, four-fifths of our servants are Irish—liars and dirty . . . Your Irish immigrant at eight and ten shillings a week has as often as not never been inside any other household than her native hovel, and stares in astonishment to find that you don't keep a pig on your drawing-room sofa. On entering your house, she gapes in awe of what she considers the grandeur around her, and the whole of her first day's work consists of ejaculating 'Lor' and 'Goodness!' We once had a hopeful of this kind who, after she had been given full instructions as to how a rice-pudding was to be made, sat down and wept bitterly for half an hour, till—her mistress having told her to 'bake'—the happy thought struck her to put a dish full of rice in the oven, *sans* milk, *sans* eggs, *sans* everything. Another Biddy, engaged by a friend of ours, having to make a yeast-cake, put it under her bed-clothes 'just to plump it a bit.' A third, having been given a bill-of-fare for the day put soup, meat, and pudding all into one pot, and served them up *au pot-pourri*.

In truth, it was probably Mr Twopenny who was rather stupid. Bound to work out a contract, or unable to earn a living in any other way, 'biddies' such as these subverted their master's authority in whatever way they could. Feigning stupidity was a favourite tactic; it spared one work and generally enabled one to avoid the worst of the master's wrath. Indeed, under the guise of stupidity servants often punished their masters, scorching shirts or burning roasts. This form of protest was once practised by the convicts, and was developed by the servants intended to take their place. In each case it was an attempt to regain a sense of dignity and identity in an otherwise harsh and brutal life.

(See Document 2.4.)

Conditions for live-in domestic servants changed little from one century to another. The introduction of labour-saving machinery to the home brought them little benefit. A gas stove was easier to handle than a wood-burning one, but employers expected a far more elaborate meal to compensate for their investment. With the vacuum cleaner came demands for a higher standard of cleanliness. Electric light revealed dust and dirt far more readily than candles. Changes to the industry itself also added to the workload. From the early 1900s, domestic service ceased to be a specialised profession; a general maid now took on the chores of laundress, seamstress, lady's maid and cleaner. She could do so because her mistress had become a housewife. The industrialisation of the home meant that housework had become respectable. Now even the finest of ladies could cook and clean and yet not soil their clothes or ruin their complexions. But maid and mistress toiling together did little to alter their relationship. Familiarity bred contempt and employers (fearful of a fall in status) insisted

Reconstruct the conversation between this colonial mistress and her cook.

(*Boomerang*, 12 January 1889, p. 10)

DOCUMENT 2.4

In the editor's opinion

The old saying that life is made up of small worries is well illustrated by the complaint of our recent correspondent "A Harassed Housekeeper," who brings under notice one of the most annoying features of the servant-girl question. The suggested formation of a domestic "employers' union" to resist the unreasonable claims of the Bridget of the day, opens up an enticing prospect of escape from the present thraldom of the enterprising young woman who wants the highest wages, combined with regular and frequent "nights out," a whole holiday at least once a month, and various other accompaniments of liberal living. But, unfortunately, the idea is too Utopian for realisation in the existing state of society, though there is no knowing to what lengths the nominal mistress of the house may be driven when the Domestic Servants' Union of which we heard so much not long ago has found its feet. Meanwhile, however, it may console "A "Harassed Housekeeper," and a good many others in like plight, to know that employers are not, as our correspondent supposes "without redress" in cases where domestic servants engage with a mistress and afterwards "throw her "over" for another and more agreeable situation. Domestic servants are expressly included by the interpretation clause in the Masters and Servants Act, which provides that where any servant contracts in writing with any person to serve for any time or in any manner, and does not enter into or commence the service according to contract, a penalty of three months' imprisonment may be indicted. If the agreement is verbal only, no punishment is provided for unless an advance on account of wages has been obtained by the servant. Seeing that the custom at servants' registry offices is invariably to draw up a written contract between employer and servant, the provisions of the act would in general apply to the constantly-recurring trouble complained of. It is only necessary that someone should have the courage to issue a summons and attend a police court — not a very formidable affair — and so make an example of a delinquent, and the cure of at any rate one household grievance would be effected.

(*Argus*, 4 November 1890)

• What 'remedy' does the *Argus* editor suggest for the servant problem? What does this suggest about attitudes of the time?

on deference and obedience from their servants. Worst of all, a girl never escaped the eye of her employer. How could she slacken off when a mistress worked with her? How could she convince an employer that some chores were more difficult than others? The increasing tendency towards antagonism between maid and mistress poisoned the home life of many middle-class families. A child of ten in 1917, Barbara Falk recalled the day when a servant struck back at her employers:

It was a breathless humid summer evening, our nurse's day out. Mother had read the story in the garden. It was my turn to go to bed first. 'Go and ask Mabel to put you to bed,' Mother said after a dutiful kiss. Prolonging the walk to the front door by taking small reluctant steps into the empty silent house, through the swing door, from quiet carpet to linoleum. Where was Mabel? She wasn't in the nurseries. A timid tap on the kitchen door and a peep in. Nobody there. Where could she be?

Suddenly the house became an enveloping menace, and I began to run—out the back door on to the porch, and there was Mabel in her uniform with the stiff collar, fanning herself and fondling the panting dog. 'Please, Mabel, mother says will you put me to bed.' And then the fury was unleashed.

'Am I never to have a moment's peace? You and your mother! I've slaved for your family all these years, and see what you've done to me! Yes, you! You and your mother! Look at that!' she shouted, thrusting her right hand at me. Three of the fingers must have been broken and badly set. It was an ugly maimed claw, and I had done it.

'Go to your room!'

The bath she poured was so hot that it burned, and when Mabel put her hand in to wash me, there was new anger:

'You should have told me! Boiling yourself! For that you'll have your bath cold! You'll get me into trouble!'

It was all my fault. I'd broken her fingers and now I ought to have said the bath was scalding me.

But there was more to come.

'Have you emptied your bladder?'

What did it mean? 'Yes,' I answered miserably. But when I was in bed I had an agonising need for the toilet and began to cry.

'What is it now?'

'My tooth is hurting.'

'I'll get your mother!'

And so I was saved by a lie, comforted, stuff rubbed on a tooth, and a chamber-pot provided.

(See Document 2.5.)

Work outside

No comfort came for the likes of Mabel. Placed in intolerable situations, many live-in servants quit the families they had served faithfully. Most found work in outside institutions: hospitals, 'homes' or boarding houses, hotels and the expanding catering industry. Cecilia Shelley was typical of many. At sixteen she escaped the 'prison life' of a private domestic and drifted from one situation to another. For five years or more she worked in boarding houses, hotels and tearooms, dreaming of the day she would save enough money to cross the ocean.

Some situations were better than others. Boarding houses were often run by women whose husbands or parents had died. Untrained for anything else, all they could do was rent out rooms in the homes they lived in. Most of the boarding houses that Cecilia worked in were old, run-down and 'crawling with cockroaches', and their owners generally employed only one or two servants to help them. The hotel industry, by contrast, was wealthy and expanding. 'Three meals a day and a good bed' was, in Cecilia's experience, the promise of every publican. But Cecilia never earnt enough to leave the city she was born in. All these jobs paid a pittance and worked women like Cecilia to exhaustion. A tearoom in Perth was the 'worst of all damn places'.

With the aid of a DOMESTIC and Attachments any housewife can do her work better and in one-twentieth the time.

This advertisement for an early-model vacuum cleaner foreshadows the demise of the human 'domestic' after which it is named. To what extent were such appliances really 'labour-saving' for middle-class housewives?

(Mitchell Library, State Library of New South Wales)

Opposite: *Gouge Pty Ltd cleaning and dyeing factory, Melbourne. The industrialisation of domestic tasks such as cleaning moved work from the home to the factory. Which of the tasks depicted here are performed by men?*

(*Argus*, Week-end Magazine, 12 November 1938)

DOCUMENT 2.5

'The maid's point of view'

The Problem of the

Servant Girl

The article by Marie E. J. Pitt in a recent number of "The Lone Hand," dealing with the present chaos in domestic service, has resulted in an extraordinary rain of letters to the Editor. As the subject, despite the gibes of the comic artists, is really an important one, we publish three of the articles received.

I.—*The Domestic Servant's Point of View*

By A DOMESTIC SERVANT

I AM a domestic, and am thus qualified to speak on this important question from the maid's point of view. From my own experience—which has certainly not been too pleasant—I have come to the conclusion that we are not properly treated, through being misunderstood and also because we will not speak up for ourselves. I was afraid to speak myself when I first went out into the world.

Here are a few suggestions that would not be considered unreasonable by any well thinking mistress, and that would not be difficult to have carried out. I will mention where one maid only is kept, and begin with the bedroom. A mistress should not forget it is the only room in her usually well furnished house we may call our own. It is usually off the kitchen. We do not mind that in the least, provided it is nice and comfortable—by being comfortable I mean a proper bed and bedding, one easy chair, and the usual necessary bedroom furniture. We are not asking for a wardrobe, but please do have something erected in one corner of the room where we may hang our clothes. A few pieces of timber and a little art muslin would not cost much, nor would it to have the floor nicely covered.

Then there is the food. A mistress should certainly see that we have enough and proper food. I have had to buy my own food very often. I had not the same food that was sent into the dining-room; a very inferior quality was ordered for the kitchen. We should also have time to eat our food. The cap is another objection. I think a mistress should allow a maid to choose her own—the objection is, I think, to a certain kind of cap, especially the streamers, which are most ugly. Thank Providence, they are dying out, and old-fashioned; the bow is the prettiest trade mark, if girls must wear them.

I consider the bathroom is one of the most important matters. In some houses the maids are provided with this convenience; the majority are without. I remember asking one mistress, after I had been at her house for two or three days, if the maids had a bathroom. Imagine my disgust when she informed me the girls used one of the laundry tubs. I could not help remarking then that that meant I should have to wait till she was out before I could use her bath. I got permission to use it then, and a bathroom was built straight away. Two maids were kept there, and it was a doctor's house; so, you see, if we do not speak we have to put up with it.

We object to the long hours. Who would not? In some cases we are going from 6 a.m. till 10 p.m. If we are not working all the time, we are expected to be on hand and ready for every call till then. Ten hours are quite sufficient for any maid to be on duty—some are not as strong as others. It would not be so objectionable if we had a proper holiday occasionally; at present we are working all the week, and only a few hours (two or three sometimes) either on Saturday or Sunday to look forward to. In many houses the maids are allowed a half-day weekly, and a whole day every four weeks. Why doesn't every mistress grant the latter holiday? Is it selfishness, or want of thought? I must not forget to add the half-day begins very often after three o'clock, and the whole day at twelve o'clock. We are not satisfied with that. If a mistress would help, not hinder—as is often the case—and see that we get out at two o'clock instead of four, we would study her more; but the present continual drudging, fourteen hours sometimes, day after day, and no regular holiday to look for except a few hours after rushing round and cramming a whole day's work into a half-day, are conditions about which we cannot help complaining.

Many think the work is degrading. It cannot be wondered at when we are subjected to so much unnecessary ridicule; but we will put up with that if we are treated fairly. We are called ignorant and badly brought up because we will not humble ourselves. Australians will never do that. A mistress should be quite satisfied if she possess a refined and domesticated girl without enforcing unpleasant duties upon her, such as, "Yes, master," "No, master," "Yes, ma'am." I inquired of one mistress why she was so particular on this point. She replied, the master did not like undue familiarity from the servants. What are we if we are not even fit to use their name? I told her I thought the undue familiarity came from their side. We understood each other; and that duty was not enforced; and I was never treated as an inferior again in that house. They were most kind to me.

A mistress, I am sure, would have no trouble in keeping her maids if she would, to the best of her ability, carry out a few, if not all, of these suggestions. There would be no need for a union, though it is a splendid idea, if only to bring girls in closer contact with each other. There are many State children and orphans who are domestics. I think sometimes what a lonely and a hard life they must have. Through a union we may perhaps help others who are less fortunate than ourselves. The cause of a lot of domestic trouble is in the uncalled-for interference of people who cannot keep maids themselves, through their own fault, but who will persist in dictating to a better natured person how they should treat their girls. Where there are two or more maids kept a mistress would not find it difficult to comply with all these suggestions; and there would certainly be more satisfaction for herself and maids.

(*Lone Hand*, 2 October 1911)

- Why does 'A Domestic Servant' think service 'un-Australian'? Had conditions for domestic servants improved over time?

It was a grim . . . place because the war was on. It was grim. Twenty-two and sixpence we got; we bought our own uniforms. I had a room in Perth, no breakfast and I couldn't afford a cup of tea. When you got to work, you'd look around for a crust of bread and sometimes we'd steal a cup of tea and nearly choke when the manager would come down and catch us drinking it! Then at lunch-time, we had a meal for a girl—two bits of meat with gravy around it, and a potato and sometimes a green. That was our dinner and nothing at night-time.

(See Document 2.6.)

Serving tea under these conditions was hard enough, but pulling a beer posed problems all of its own. Barmaids, then as today, were hired on the basis of looks and personality: publicans considered that a handsome friendly young woman was needed at the bar to entice men from their families. One barmaid's daughter remembered her mother's work as a form of prostitution:

'The proposition'—barmaid and customer.

(*Boomerang*, 13 December 1890)

Y OUNG FREDDY stands before the bar
  Whence all but he have fled ;
The smoke from Freddy's big cigar
  Forms circles round his head.
A rose-bud blushes on his coat,
  His heart is full of joy,
And many simple signs denote
  He is a Barmaid's "Boy."

Behind the bar Miss Flossy stands ;
  The girl is slim and dark,
And washing glasses gives her hands
  A kind of ruddy bark ;
But ah ! she is a graceful dear,
  So fresh and trim and smart :
Not stout and bitter like the beer—
  Although a little "tart."

Young Freddy stops a solid hour
  To gaze in Flossy's eyes,
And soon the rosebud from his coat
  Upon her bosom lies ;
He swallows half-a-dozen drinks
  With rapture and delight,
At last the wearied syren thinks
  "It's time to say good-night."

His fingers Flossy's fingers press—
  How thrilling is their touch !—
He'd like to snatch a fond caress,
  But Flossy knows too much.
(Of all the womenkind we meet,
  There's none can be so coy,
So altogether quite discreet,
  As barmaids with a Boy.)

Young Freddy takes a fond farewell,
  And struts away on air
(Who knows the power of barmaid's spell,
  Unless he has "been there"?)
Another Boy comes strolling in
  As Freddy turns his back ;
That rosebud, fastened with a pin,
  Brings happiness to Jack.

Then Flossy hears it all again,
  For Jack is also young,
And sings the old familiar strain
  Which foolish Fred has sung ;
And, after Jack, on Dick and Tom
  Her arts she must employ—
There is no rest for Flossy from
  The ardent Barmaid's Boy.

They come and go, they go and come—
  Boys dull, or bright and quick :
She hardly gives a thought to some—
  The others turn her sick ;
Mechanical the witching glance
  She sheds on all the batch,
And Floss ignores each decent chance
  To make a decent match.

She might have Bertie if she chose,
  The notion makes her smile ;
And as for Freddy, goodness knows
  He's not at all her style ;
Such youngsters may be straight and true,
  As some among them are—
They haven't learned the way to woo
  Young ladies at the bar.

For all their roses and their gloves
  The girl cares not a jot,
One man, in truth, the syren loves,
  A lazy, reckless sot ;
Pert, pretty Flossy's peace of mind
  Her "fancy" will destroy—
The Barmaid is at least as blind
  As any Barmaid's Boy.

And, doubtless, after many days
  (When Freddy and the rest
Have settled down to sober ways
  And given barmaids best),
To Floss, in Time's hard lesson schooled,
  This thought will oft occur :
That, while her Boys she lightly fooled,
  Her "chap" was fooling *her*.
                    EDMUND FISHER.

(*Bulletin*, 20 December 1890)

Both illustrations and the poem emphasise the sexuality of barmaids in relation to their customers.

DOCUMENT 2.6

A Sydney waitress

At that moment a waitress who had been arranging the next table came and took her place against the wall close behind Nellie. Such an opportunity to talk unionism was not to be lost, so Nellie unceremoniously dropped her conversation with Ned and enquired, as before stated, into the becapped girl's hours. The waitress was tall and well-featured, but sallow of skin and growing haggard, though barely 20, if that. Below her eyes were bluish hollows. She suffered plainly from the disorders caused by constant standing and carrying, and at this end of her long week was in evident pain.

• • • •

'You're not allowed to talk either?' she asked the waitress, when the manager had disappeared.

'No. They're very strict. You get fined if you're seen chatting to customers and if you're caught resting. And you get fined if you break anything, too. One girl was fined six shillings last week.'

'Why do you stand it? If you were up in our part of the world we'd soon bring 'em down a notch or two.' This from Ned.

'Out in the bush it may be different,' said the girl, identifying his part of the world by his dress and sunburnt face. 'But in towns you've got to stand it.'

'Couldn't you girls form a union?' asked Nellie.

'What's the use, there's plenty to take our places.'

'But if you were all in a union there wouldn't be enough.'

'Oh, we can't trust a lot of girls. Those who live at home and just work to dress themselves are the worst of the lot. They'd work for ten shillings or five.'

'But they'd be ashamed to blackleg if once they were got into the union,' persisted Nellie. 'It's worth trying, to get a rise in wages and to stop fining and have shorter hours and seats while you're waiting.'

'Yes, it's worth trying if there was any chance. But there are so many girls. You're lucky if you get work at all now and just have to put up with anything. If we all struck they could get others to-morrow.'

'But not waitresses. How'd they look here, trying to serve dinner with a lot of green hands?' argued Nellie. 'Besides, if you had a union, you could get a lot without striking at all. They know now you can't strike, so they do just exactly as they like.'

'They'd do what they—' began the waitress. Then she broke off with another 's-s-s' as the manager crossed the room again.

'They'd do what they like, anyway,' she began once more. 'One of our girls was in the union the Melbourne waitresses started. They had a strike at one of the big restaurants over the manager insulting one of the girls. They complained to the boss and wanted the manager to apologise, but the boss wouldn't listen and said they were getting very nice. So at dinner time, when the bell rang, they all marched off and put on their hats. The customers were all waiting for dinner and the girls were all on strike and the boss nearly went mad. He was going to have them all arrested, but when the gentlemen heard what it was about they said the girls were right and if the manager didn't apologise they'd go to some other restaurant always. So the manager went to the girl and apologised.'

'By gum!' interjected Ned. 'Those girls were hummers.'

'I suppose the boss victimised afterwards?' asked Nellie, wiser in such matters.

'That's just it,' said the girl, in a disheartened tone. 'In two or three weeks every girl who'd had anything to do with stirring the others up was bounced for something or other. The manager did what he liked afterwards.'

(William Lane, [John Miller, pseud.], *A Workingman's Paradise*, Edward Dunlop & Co., Sydney, 1892, pp. 28–30)

• Ned and Nellie are the central characters in William Lane's novel, *A Workingman's Paradise*, set in Sydney in the late nineteenth century. It is a rare and sensitive study of women's working lives. What does their conversation with the waitress reveal about her wages and conditions? Why is it so difficult to unionise this work-force? What sort of 'insult' was the manager of the restaurant likely to have made?

In the early days, women were generally barmaids if they had nothing else they could do and if they were attractive. I suppose you had to have some ability because you had to count the drink out. But it was really being good-looking . . . the women were supposed to oblige the men. If pressure was put on some women to keep their jobs, they became . . . willing victims . . . obliging the men customers. Women held their jobs better if they were obliging. It's the same now in certain walks of life. Sometimes the barmaids were sacked if they weren't obliging, not if they weren't efficient.

(See Document 2.7.)

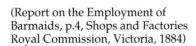

DOCUMENT 2.7

The sweetest and fairest

[As] soon as a girl gets rather faded in one house she goes to a house of a lower grade, and down and down, until no publican will have her. The next time you will find her knocking about Lonsdale-street or Little Bourke-street. Then she goes amongst the Chinamen; from thence to the hospital, and then into the grave.

• • • •

Wanted, a beautiful barmaid,
 To serve at a City bar
A plain-looking girl would mar trade,
 And would prove too slow by far.
Her eyes must be blue as a violet,
 Or as black as a jetty sloe;
But they must not be over modest,
 But sparkle, and burn and glow!

Wanted, a beautiful barmaid,
 To shine in a drinking den
To entrap the youth of the nation,
 And ruin the City men;
To brighten destruction's pathway,
 False gleams with dark fate to blend;
To stand near Despair dark gateway,
 To hide Sin's sad bitter end.

Wanted, a beautiful barmaid,
 To serve in a drinking store;
A girl who's an adept at witching,
 Who has served in the trade before,
Gifted with beauty the rarest,
 To garnish a drinking den,
And who is the sweetest and fairest,
 To ruin the City men!

(Report on the Employment of Barmaids, p.4, Shops and Factories Royal Commission, Victoria, 1884)

(Archdeacon Boyce, reproduced in Keith Dunstan, *Wowsers*, Cassell, Melbourne, 1968, p. 79)

• Archdeacon Boyce was a founding member of the Local Option League of New South Wales, a group determined to restrict the sale of intoxicating liquor. Why does he depict the barmaid as the agent of men's ruin? What do these accounts suggest about the 'qualifications' required of a barmaid?

In such walks of life, walking out was probably the only solution. Thousands of domestic servants, Eleanor included, left their work to establish families of their own, finding it preferable to work in their own kitchens than the kitchens of others. Those who could not leave strived to build a better life for their children. The barmaid's daughter never had to prostitute herself at a bar: her mother's work paid her way to an exclusive girls' school. And Cecilia Shelley eventually struck back at the meanness of her employers. In the early 1920s she called on the workers to 'down their mops' and strike for better wages. As she recalled 'it was *Miss* Shelley from that day on'; her work as a union organiser brought not just better wages but the dignity which domestic service had denied her.

Cecilia Shelley was not the first woman to unionise domestic servants: forty years earlier Rose Summerfield, socialist, feminist and free thinker, was appointed women's organiser for the Australian Workers Union. Throughout the hot summer of 1892–1893 she toured eastern Australia, addressing audiences as far afield as Melbourne and Bourke. That was an achievement in itself; the citizens of Bourke had never before been addressed by a woman, let alone one who called on her sisters to 'recognise their worth':

You sew beautiful garments for others to wear, you stitch, stitch, stitch from morning to night for others' comfort, you wash and scrub and clean while others are idle . . . you have brains to think, you have hands to work, strength and energy and concentration . . . then surely you have a right, the indispensable right to fair and just compensation . . . for your daily [labour].

But for Summerfield unionism meant much more than better wages and conditions. Once a woman had escaped her 'economic thraldom' she could 'take her place as the mate and equal of man'. As such her style of unionism was particularly attentive to women's needs. Summerfield advocated the creation of creches for women who had to earn a living, arguing that child-care was a legitimate union concern. She supported the establishment of women's cooperatives, where laundresses and seamstresses could work free of the supervision of men.

Summerfield was a woman before her time; perhaps it is not surprising that none of her projects succeeded. By 1894, the women's union was abandoned, a casualty of economic depression and the myriad difficulties which confronted an organiser of women's trades. Despairing of the prejudices of a male-dominated union movement, Summerfield left Australia for William Lane's utopian colony in Paraguay. Her conclusion held true for a generation of women organisers: only free of capitalism and patriarchy could women be more than 'mere machines'.

Not all women needed to escape the servitude of service. Thousands preferred work with a machine to work with 'any bloody mistress'. It is to the factories and workshops that we must turn for their story.

Notes

Reynold Johns, Florrie Robinson—Based on Reynold Johns' diary in the La Trobe Library, Victoria (MS 10075).

R. E. N. Twopenny—*Town Life in Australia*, Elliot Stock, 1883, p. 51.

Barbara Falk—'The unpayable debt', in P. Grimshaw and L. Strahan, *The Half-Open Door*, Hale & Iremonger, Sydney, 1982, pp. 21–2.

Cecilia Shelley—Jan Carter, *Nothing to Spare: Reflections of Australian Pioneering Women*, Penguin, Ringwood, 1986, pp. 97–8.

Rose Summerfield—*Commonweal*, 4 February 1891.

SUGGESTIONS FOR STUDY

For discussion

1 Of all the jobs done by domestic servants in the nineteenth century, which do you think would have been the hardest?
2 Would it have been better to be the only servant of a family such as the Johns family, or one of a number of domestic staff in a larger and wealthier household?
3 What kinds of domestic work required skill?
4 What sorts of girls became domestic servants?
5 Who had more power in this employer–employee relationship?
6 How did labour-saving domestic appliances affect the work of servants?
7 In the twentieth century domestic servants were employed increasingly by hotels, restaurants and boarding houses rather than private homes. Do you think these workers were better off than those in private homes?

To write about

1 Cecilia Shelley organised a union of hotel and catering staff to try to improve their pay and conditions.
   a Write a leaflet she might have distributed urging workers to join the union.
   b Write a statement she might have made to the newspapers explaining the unionists' grievances.
2 Australian employers frequently lamented the lack of good domestic servants. Write a dialogue between two nineteenth-century middle-class ladies discussing 'the servant problem'.
3 Draw up the weekly schedule of a live-in domestic servant in the late 1880s. What are her responsibilities? How much of her time can be considered her own?
4 Make a list of the labour-saving devices used in your home. What functions did each of these replace? Which labour-saving devices preceded them? When were they invented, who used them and why?

Community resources
The historic home

1 Visit an historic home in your area, one classified by the National Trust or managed by the local museum. Draw up a floor plan of the house in question. In which areas did men and women work? If possible, note the amount of living space allocated for employer and employee.
2 How many servants did the house employ? What did they do and how did the employer–employee ratio change over time? The names of the owners of the house are probably carefully recorded; have you been able to find out any of their servants' names?
3 What would the lady of the house have done in her spare time? What contribution did she make to the day-to-day running of the home?
4 Inspect the exhibits. Great care is usually taken to preserve the furniture and heirlooms of the house's owners; is the same care taken to preserve the possessions of its employees? What working implements are on display? Who used them and how were they used?
5 Working in groups of two, have one student act the role of a female reporter from the 1990s who has travelled back in time to the late 1880s. The reporter interviews a female domestic servant (the other student). Research each role carefully, including the questions to be asked by the reporter. You have five minutes to conduct the interview in front of the class or on video.

3 Manufacturing

The clothing trades

Louisa O'Neil, born into an Irish working-class family in Brunswick around 1900, found that life offered her few career opportunities. 'The only thing I ever heard about what you do', she recalled, 'was become a seamstress, or go to tailoring (and this is what I went to) and learn a trade'.

In Brunswick, Louisa was close to the centre of Victoria's clothing trade. With fares expensive, people tried to find work within walking distance of their homes. Surrounded by clothing factories, it is not surprising that Louisa saw no other option than to work in this industry when the time came for her to earn a living. But her comment would have been true for thousands of other young Australian women at that time, even those who did not live so close to clothing workrooms.

Almost half a century had passed since Eleanor Hargreaves took her first job, and the female job market had changed considerably. Whereas Eleanor was typical of her generation of young single women in going into domestic service, Louisa represented the growing number of girls who chose to work in a factory. In Victoria in 1901, for instance, about a quarter of all female workers were employed in manufacturing, and of these the overwhelming majority (over 90 per cent) were involved in making clothing and textiles. After the gold rushes of the 1850s, local industries such as clothing and food processing expanded quickly to supply the large number of immigrants who had come to Australia in search of gold. But these industries supplied not only boots and clothes, biscuits and jam; they also offered women seeking work the first real alternative to domestic service. Perth, Brisbane and Hobart were slower to industrialise than Melbourne, Sydney and Adelaide, but by the end of the nineteenth century those cities too had factory work to offer their women.

(See Document 3.1.)

Not all the women who went to work in these industries were like Louisa: a working-class girl whose factory earnings were an essential contribution to the economic survival of her family.

Girls and boys in factories

Boys are far too independent . . . the troubles experienced in this matter are so great that in many factories boy labour is entirely dispensed with, and girls, who are found to be just as quick and much more attentive, employed in their stead.

• • • •

Cynical naturalists tell us that there are three animals whose natures are always in opposition—namely a pig, a hen and a woman . . . In justification to the cynic, I must say that it requires a good piece of domestic diplomacy to get a woman to do what you wish. Every married man knows the truth of this remark . . . Don't appoint a big, clumsy lout of a man as overseer of machinists and fitters . . . or you will have half your girls in tears and the other half as obstinate as mules, which, in either case, means a great loss of time.

(Report of Chief Inspector of Factories, Victoria, 1889, p. 5)

• Do you think factory inspectors in the 1990s would make the same judgment?

('Boot Factory Management', in *Australian Leather Journal*, 15 October 1902, p. 370)

• What special problems were girls seen as presenting to factory managers, and how does this writer suggest they be overcome?

Some kinds of clothing manufacture attracted a quite different class of worker: young women from more middle-class homes who hoped to learn enough in a workroom to enable them to make their own dresses and hats. Although they helped their families' budgets by reducing the cost of their own clothing, their labour in the workrooms was often unpaid. They were content to work for nothing so long as they could enjoy the companionship of other workers and learn a few useful skills. While this was all very well for those who did not need cash so desperately, it meant that the large number of girls who were working for the money also had to accept positions which initially paid nothing at all, or at most a mere two shillings and sixpence per week. For someone like Eleanor, who had to earn straight away, this meant that the biggest section of the clothing industry was closed to her. However, for women who could survive the poorly paid apprenticeship period, and who were fortunate enough to work for an employer who gave them good training, dressmaking could provide a relatively well-paid occupation. This was especially so at the more exclusive end of the trade, where workers were making up clothes for society ladies.

(See Documents 3.2 and 3.3.)

Other types of clothing work could also provide a bare living for a single woman, or sometimes even a degree of comfort. Women who sewed men's ready-to-wear suits and trousers in factories could usually earn up to twice as much, for instance, as women like

Eleanor who sewed shirts and underclothing. Order tailoresses—women who made men's suits to fit each individual customer—could earn even more.

Some of the best paid jobs in the industry were, however, reserved for men; women were not usually taught to cut and press men's clothing, and were rarely allowed to make the best quality men's frockcoats. Edna Ryan, who was one of eleven children in a struggling working-class Sydney family, had three older sisters who each entered a different section of the clothing trade early in the twentieth century. Their experiences reflect some of the diversity which this industry offered.

(Evidence of Mrs Agnes Milne, shirtmaker)

DOCUMENT 3.2

Shirtmaking in Adelaide

4062.   Do you think people can make a fair livelihood out of this work? — Not at all.

4063.   Are there many people, nevertheless, engaged in it? — Yes; scores. No honest person can make a fair living out of it. Still there are scores who do make a good living out of it.

4064.   How, by scamping the work? — Well, there are various ways. I called on a woman who said she made a very good thing out of it, and was quite surprised I joined the Working Women's Trades Union. She said I had no right to do it as I was a sub-contractor. Ever since I have done this work I have worked myself with my girls, and I have never been able to make it pay.

4065.   How do you suggest that these people who try to make out that it pays achieve those results? — One way is by getting a number of little girls, under 14, and paying them 2s.6d. a week for six months. Another way is by a sub-contractor getting so much stuff over out of the material supplied to him after he has cut out the specified number of shirts. Sometimes he has two or three yards over. Also by grinding the flesh and blood out of the girls they make it pay.

4066.   You say by remunerating girls at the rate you pay no better results can be gained than you have told us of? — No.

4067.   I suppose your rates are as high as any which are paid? — Yes.

4068.   And they are not very remunerative? — If the girls who work with me had not homes they could not live on the money.

4943.   *By Mr. McPherson* — What do the general average of those employed in shirt-making get per week? — About 10s. I do not think there are any who get more than 15s. — not by working nine hours a day.

4944.   Do you think 10s. is sufficient to enable women to live decently and honestly? — No; I do not think any reasonable being would think so.

4945.   How many earning these wages have to live entirely upon this amount, or are there a fair proportion who live with their parents? — The greater portion live with their parents.

4946.   Do you think, nevertheless, there is a percentage who have to live upon 10s. or 15s a week? — Yes.

4947.   Do you know any instances of girls who have suffered ill-health through having to work excessively long hours, and in insanitary places, at this class of work? — I know of several who are in poor health, and who blame it to the work. We do not blame the surroundings of these places so much as the hard work at machines for the injuries.

4948.   Do you know any actual cases of your own knowledge? — I know of one girl who has had to give up on account of the hard work.

4949.   Do you know any more? — I know of some who failed in health, and who, having gone away for a time, are back again better.

4950.   In the particular case you refer to, do you think the ill-health was caused by having to work long hours and in an insanitary building? — Yes; and in being driven so at the work.

DOCUMENT 3.2 CONTINUED

2137.   *By the Chairman* — You do needlework? — Yes; I take in needlework of all kinds.
2138.   How long have you been engaged in that business? — Over two years — that is, since I have taken the shopwork. I have been at dressmaking for many years.
2139.   What do you mean by shop work? — I mean shirt work and slop factory work.
2140.   Do you do much at it? — I have had to get a living for all of us lately. My husband has been ill.
2141.   Do you employ many hands? — Only two girls.
2142.   Do you work yourself? — Yes.
2143.   What age are the girls? — The elder one is 18 and the other is 15.
2144.   Are they any relation to yourself? No.
2145.   Have you had the two hands all the time you have taken in shop work? — No; one has been with me twelve months and the other seven.
2146.   Have you had other hands during that time? — When I did all shirts I had eight girls working for me, but so low was the pay that I had to give it up.
2147.   How long ago did you have to give it up? — It is about twelve months since I gave up the shirt work with so many girls.
2148.   But you still do shirt work? — Yes; but I am working for the sweaters now.
2149.   What ages were the eight girls? — I could not tell.
2150.   Were they very young? — Oh, no; there were none very young. None under 15.
2151.   Was that the average age? — Yes. Two were 18 or 19.
2152.   You say you work for the sweaters now? — Yes.
2153.   Whom do you refer to as sweaters? — Well, those who take work from the firms and cut it out and give it to us after it is cut out.
2154.   What do you mean by sweating? — I call it sweating when 6s. a dozen is given to the one cutting out the shirt, and they give us no more than $3\frac{1}{2}$d. for each shirt to make it, fold it, and press it.
2155.   You complain bitterly of the rate of wage you receive from the persons who let you have the shirts they take from the shop? — Yes.
2156.   Do the large clothing factories give the work out to these sweaters? — The work comes from the warehouses. We get it from them at the rate of three or four dozen at a time, and carry them home.

2180.   Are you doing any now? Yes; because I am obliged to do it. My husband is sick, and I have four children to keep. There is no other work. I could not get dressmaking, and I was obliged to accept the shirts. I have made fourteen dozen a week at 2s. 6d. a dozen.
2181.   Including cotton? — No; cotton was found.
2182.   Who finds the buttons? — They belong to the material and come from the warehouse.
2183.   I understand you to complain of the price as being insufficient for the work done? — Yes.
2184.   Is there any other grievance in connection with the factory work that you would like to point out? — No. I have never worked in a factory myself.
2185.   You said you and your girls turned out fourteen dozen shirts in a week? — Yes.
2186.   What hours did you work? — I worked sometimes from 7.30 in the morning to 12 and 1 in the next morning. My girls did not work that time.
2187   You had intervals for meals? — Yes.

2224.   Could you earn so much money by going to the factory as you do at your own home? — I do not suppose I could, because working at home I work longer hours. At the factory they would not give me more than 12s. a week.
2225.   You earn more than that at home? — Yes.
2226.   What would be your average weekly wage now? — By working night and day I make in some weeks 14s. I am not all the time at my machine. I have my family to attend to. That is why I work such late hours at night. There are dozens round me who have to do the same. There are some who have to work at 2s. 6d. a dozen single stitch. Mine is single stitch.

(Evidence of Elizabeth Rogers, needlewoman, minutes of evidence, Shops and Factories Royal Commission, Adelaide, 1892, vol. 2)

• What do these extracts from the evidence to a royal commission in 1892 reveal about the kinds of people engaged in shirtmaking, the circumstances in which they worked and the pay they received for their labours?

DOCUMENT 3.3

Unskilled workers?

The worst paid type of clothing work was 'finishing'—sewing on buttons and making button-holes, attaching hooks and eyes, hemming and generally tidying up the garment. The low rates of pay were usually explained by reference to the unskilled nature of the work. But, as an official inquiry found, it was not as clear-cut as that:

To call them unskilled is not quite correct, for the work of finishing often requires the possession of expertness and ability on the part of the operative which can only be acquired after long practice.

(Shops and Factories Royal Commission, 1893, Victoria, First Report, p. 13)

• What does this royal commission report mean by 'skill'? What other possible ways are there of defining skill? How far do wages today reflect different levels of skill?

Three sewing sisters

Christina started work in 1905 at Cromar's Costumieres, a firm which made women's skirt and coat suits. For the first six months she was paid nothing, then two shillings sixpence each week. The twenty machinists sat each side of a long bench-table facing each other. A talented singer, Christina was allowed to sing in the workroom providing there were no customers about. Once trained, she earned about twenty-five shillings a week.

Hannah was a machinist in the tailoring trade, starting work in 1907. Unlike Christina, she moved from one firm to another. She left one place because the foreman would not allow the workers to speak to each other—they were to knock on the table and point to the article they wanted. After putting up with this for a while, she could finally stand it no longer and threw some reels of cotton at the foreman. Other foremen were too familiar and in such cases she walked out rather than put up with sexual harassment. In 1915 she was making soldiers' overcoats on huge power-machines. Her arms ached from the weight of the heavy material so she left this job for a lighter one. Hannah was paid piecework according to a list of rates set by the arbitration award, but she never earned more than twenty shillings a week.

Neither Christina nor Hannah had any chance of learning the better-paid work of cutting or pressing. This work was done by men in a separate room, which the girls were forbidden to enter.

Victoria became a 'top dog' in the trade—a coat-hand, making quality men's coats to fit individual customers. She was taught by male tailors in small high-class firms in the city and earned much more than her sisters. As Edna Ryan put it, 'Victoria really made a man-size contribution to the household'. As well as her daytime job, she played the piano several nights a week in a local cinema. (This was in the days when silent movies were accompanied by 'mood music' from a pianist.) Victoria's earnings were especially important as she had five younger brothers and sisters not yet earning, a mother out of work and an absent father.

As the experiences of these women show, sewing was not necessarily light and respectable work. Hannah had to contend with sexual advances being made to her by men in authority. She also found machining men's overcoats very exhausting. Making women's clothing in the days of long, full dresses and lined skirts could also be very tiring, as dressmaker Lesbia Harford records in her poem, 'The Shirt Machinist':

> *I am making great big skirts*
> *For great big women—*
> *Amazons who've fed and slept*
> *Themselves inhuman.*
>
> *Such long skirts, not less than two*
> *And forty inches.*
> *Thirty round the waist for fear*
> *The webbing pinches.*
> *There must be tremendous tucks*
> *On those round bellies.*
> *Underneath the limbs will shake*
> *Like wine-soft jellies.*
>
> *I am making such big skirts*
> *And all so heavy,*
> *I can see their wearers at*
> *A lord-mayor's levee.*
> *I, who am so small and weak*
> *I have hardly grown,*
> *Wish the skirts I'm making less*
> *Unlike my own.*

The weight of the cloth was only one of the strains placed on workers. Where large numbers of sewing machines were used, conditions were particularly bad. Sewing machines had been used in Australia since the 1850s, and as more and more clothes were made ready-to-wear, more machines were used. Rather than lightening the workload, the use of sewing machines often resulted in additional stress on workers, who were expected to work so much faster. A woman who worked in some of Melbourne's factories before World War I described her experience:

The roar of the machines filling the air until it throbs again, deafening the ears and pressing on the brain like a tangible weight; the monotony of the work, and the constant effort not to fall behind with it; the endurance, both mental and physical, that must be sustained, impose a strain on the nerves none but those set down among the conditions can realise.

(See Document 3.4.)

DOCUMENT 3.4

An employer and his workers

Edward Bartlett, a clothing manufacturer employing between 100 and 350 workers (depending on the time of year), told a government inquiry in 1893 that he often swore at the girls who worked for him. But, he explained, 'I offer apologies, and we are the best of friends, it is merely a *lapsus linguae*. I never do anyone any injury.

(Evidence to Shops and Factories Royal Commission, Victoria, 1893, p. 96)

Justice H. B. Higgins, the first Chief Judge of the Commonwealth Arbitration Court, enquired into the conditions of tailoring workers in 1919 and found considerable evidence 'as to vibration, as to the artificial light, as to the strain from speed, as to the hurry, the noise, the fluffy particles, as to the long sitting and stooping, the fatigue, the frequent headaches and injury to eyesight.'

Some clothing work was less stressful and more satisfying. Women working in order workrooms, making either men's or women's clothes for individual customers, tended to find their work more enjoyable. Ruth Haynes, who worked in Collingwood, Victoria, between the wars, clearly enjoyed her work:

I worked at Foy and Gibson's in Smith Street at the men's tailoring and I got 5/- [five shillings] a week . . . I wasn't apprenticed but I learnt my trade thoroughly. It was very nice at work. We had a very nice forelady. It was homely; they weren't on your back all the time. No stopwatch on you, but you learnt your trade and the staff were all very nice.

(See Document 3.5.)

Dorothy White, who worked at a 'ready-made' factory in Flinders Lane and in the order room at Georges in Melbourne in the 1920s, found an enormous difference in the two kinds of work. She contrasted the noise and speed in 'those dreadful places' in Flinders Lane with the more leisurely and peaceful atmosphere at Georges: 'We felt very happy', she recalled, 'they really did wonderful work . . . I enjoyed the work'. Unfortunately, between 1880 and 1940 more and more clothing was made ready-to-wear, so that by the 1930s most clothing factory workers would have worked under the 'slave-driver's regime' described by Dorothy White rather than in the pleasant environment offered by firms such as Georges and Foy and Gibson.

The move to ready-made factory-produced clothing also resulted in fewer opportunities for women in the well-paid jobs of cutting/designing and managing. Whereas in the nineteenth century it was women who almost always did the designing and cutting out of dresses for their private customers, in the twentieth century this was an occupation which men took on. In fact, by the 1920s and 1930s it was quite common for dressmaking firms to

DOCUMENT 3.5

Gold or brummie

'No, it ain't brummie, Florrie. What are you givin' us? Will wouldn't give me brummie. He doesn't like to see girls wearin' it. My word, those bangles of yours are brummie, all right.'

I couldn't help thinking so, too.

'Girls are awful fond o' brummagem,' she said to me. 'You see all the rings and things they wear here. All brummie. And then they think your young man can't give you a real gold ring.

The girls were 'awful fond' of photographs, likewise. Not a day passes without the production of a piece of cardboard, with an imprint of somebody's family faces, of a picnic group, or an amatory pair. The subjects and occasions of these furnish them with plenty of conversation at a slack moment.

'Goin' to take the teapot, Jennie?'

'Yes,' said Jennie, 'in a minute.'

I wondered what was about to happen [to] the teapot, and watched it conveyed out of the room under Jennie's apron.

Presently it returned in the same position. When stood on the table, steam was issuing from the spout, and what was the portent there was no mistaking, for every girl brought her cup and had it filled.

This is tea. They don't call it afternoon tea; but, no doubt, it serves equally well in its property for cheering the company.

WORK GIRLS IN A MACINTOSH FACTORY.
(Pen-and-ink sketch by Miss Baskerville.)

The women who toil

'How many coats have you done this morning, Bella?' asked my neighbour of the girl at the machine opposite her.

'I am at my sixth,' said Bella.

'Oh, I am at the ninth.'

They are stitching leather bindings on oilskin coats.

'How are you paid for that,' I inquired.

'Sixpence a dozen the short coats, ninepence the long ones, and elevenpence for some, but that's very extra.'

'And what number can you get through in the day?'

'It all depends on the size. From two to three dozen. Think you'll stay?'

'I can't say. Is the work very hard, do you think?'

'Pretty hard. But I'd rather do it than be at home, or out at service.'

A drawer was opened by her at this juncture, and a photograph taken out. It was stealthily passed to me, under cover of her work.

'That's my family,' she informed me. 'There's mother and father in the middle, and the one nursin' the baby is my married sister. Her husband's next to her. Yes, that one's me. Think it's good? They say I look an awful fright there, as if I'd been havin' somethin' for dinner that didn't agree with me. What do you think of that young man in the corner?'

'Quite handsome,' said I, catching sight of an eager look of expectancy.

'Think so, really?'

'Yes; don't you?'

'Oh, we're goin' to be married some time.' And she turned the back of her hand, where a ring caught the light.

(Helen Davis, 'The women who toil', *New Idea*, 6 May 1903, p. 807)

- How did the workers in this macintosh factory make their workday more pleasant?

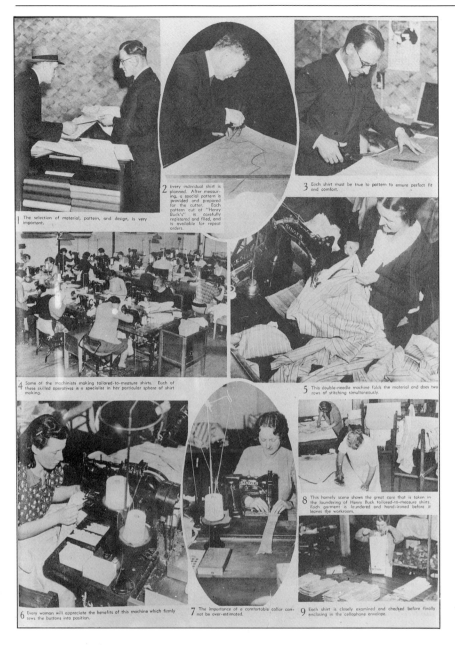

1 The selection of material, pattern, and design, is very important.

2 Every individual shirt is planned. After measuring, a special pattern is provided and prepared for the cutter. Each pattern cut at "Henry Buck's" is carefully registered and filed, and is available for repeat orders.

3 Each shirt must be true to pattern to ensure perfect fit and comfort.

4 Some of the machinists making tailored-to-measure shirts. Each of these skilled operatives is a specialist in her particular sphere of shirt making.

5 This double-needle machine folds the material and does two rows of stitching simultaneously.

6 Every woman will appreciate the benefits of this machine which firmly sews the buttons into position.

7 The importance of a comfortable collar cannot be over-estimated.

8 This homely scene shows the great care that is taken in the laundering of Henry Buck tailored-to-measure shirts. Each garment is laundered and hand-ironed before it leaves the workroom.

9 Each shirt is closely examined and checked before finally enclosing in the cellophane envelope.

These pictures clearly show the typical sexual division of labour in men's clothing factories, with men engaged in planning and cutting and women doing the sewing and ironing. Ironing damp articles such as shirts was considered entirely different to 'pressing', which involved ironing with a damp cloth over a dry garment. Pressing was men's work, and was considered 'skilled'; ironing was women's work and was regarded as unskilled.

Henry Buck Pty Ltd, Melbourne — men's order shirt firm (*Argus*, Week-end Magazine, 28 October 1939, p. 15)

Founder of the firm
Mrs E. Lucas 1848–1923

E. H. Price 1878–1945

K. H. Price 1905–   J. L. Price 1910–   E. M. Price 1907–

B. E. Price 1932–   G. T. Price 1935–

E. Lucas & Co. Pty Ltd — Pictures of generations of the firm's managing directors. A typical business progression from a female founder to a male board of directors.

(M. White, *The Golden Thread*, Melbourne, E. Lucas & Co. Pty Ltd, 1963)

employ a well-paid man to do the designing and a number of poorly-paid women to cut out as he instructed them. Although women with some money of their own could train for the designing jobs, most female cutters had little prospect of advancing. As one such woman, Gertrude Flynn, explained:

My wages are merely an existence . . . After I have paid my living expenses I have very little to spare, and not enough to pay for further tuition to enable myself to advance. To learn how to draft and design on a reliable scale requires a fair amount of money . . .

(See Documents 3.6 and 3.7.)

Men also increasingly assumed the ownership and management of the new ready-made clothing firms. All too often the reins of control passed from the original woman proprietor to sons, husbands or male boards of directors, as happened with the firm that Eleanor Lucas and her daughters had started in 1888. Sewing, which was considered almost exclusively women's work when done for nothing in the home or for small wages in a factory, became the realm of men when it became more profitable.

DOCUMENT 3.6

Sexual signals

6595.   You said women workers should be kept separate from men? — I mean tailors.

6596.   Do you think that the men in Adelaide are of such a character that it is necessary to keep the women away? — I think it is necessary anywhere. Both men and women talk about different things, and it would be injudicious to let one sex hear the conversation of the other. There are machines working in my place, but it is a different thing where there is no such noise.

6597.   If there were a law dealing with the matter, should it apply to tailors, who seem to need it especially, or factories generally? — It might apply to all.

6598.   Do you know in the Government telegraph office they have men and women? — Yes.

6599.   Do you think that should be prevented? — As far as possible.

6600.   Do you ever hear any ill results that have followed through that? — I cannot say.

6601.   Do not you think that excepting tailors people who work in factories and other places are civilised enough to be allowed to work together without any danger? — They are civilised enough; but I do not think the sexes should be mingled too much — at any rate not more than necessary.

6602.   What bad results follow? — It is difficult to describe; signals perhaps pass between them, and it is likely to lead to evil.

(Evidence of Mr W. T. McLean, tailor and manufacturer, Shops and Factories Royal Commission, South Australia, 1892)

• What kind of 'evil' do you think Mr McLean has in mind? What effect could such attitudes to mixed-sex workplaces have on women's access to employment opportunities?

DOCUMENT 3.7

Dividing the work

Certainly one of the witnesses told us of three Amazons, who were employed at [Foy and Gibson] and who did the work [of pressing] with equal efficiency to the men but the foreman there decided he would not have any more Amazons. We are with the Union there, we do not want them, we do not want to use them, or see them employed . . .

• • • •

I would not advocate that a woman should be taught the cutting, though I can cut, because we would take the bread out of the men's mouths. It is the men who cut . . .

(Evidence of Mr Read, representing the employers, Federated Clothing Trades Union of Australia vs Archer, et al., Commonwealth Court of Conciliation and Arbitration, minutes of evidence, 1919, p. 302)

(Evidence of Mrs Sarah Muir, order tailoress, Shops and Factories Royal Commission, Victoria, 1901, p. 438)

• What does the testimony of Mrs Muir and Mr Read tell us about how (and by whom) work was divided between the sexes in clothing factories?

Part of the Lucas Company's continued success lay in its diversification into textile production. These pictures show men and women at work producing new synthetic fabrics.
The sexual division of labour in the dress and lingerie section of this factory (bottom row of pictures) contrasts with that in the men's shirt factory (p. 37). What is the difference?

E. Lucas & Co. Pty Ltd, Ballarat, interior views. (*Argus,* Week-end Magazine, 9 September 1939)

Boot and shoe industry

In Melbourne, girls from Brunswick might think only of going into clothing factories, but those in suburbs such as Richmond, Clifton Hill and Collingwood had more opportunities in the boot factories which were dotted all over these inner suburbs. But while making clothes, especially women's dresses and hats, was considered suitable 'feminine' employment, this was not the case with making boots and shoes. In the nineteenth century most boot workers were males, but an increasing proportion were females employed to prepare and sew the leather shoe-uppers. Other factory workers looked down on female boot workers, possibly because they were forced to work among so many men. In reality, there was little reason for this prejudice. Men and women did completely different work within the factories and were not usually allowed

(*Boomerang*, 13 April 1889, p. 13)

• Identify the sexual division of labour in this Brisbane boot factory.

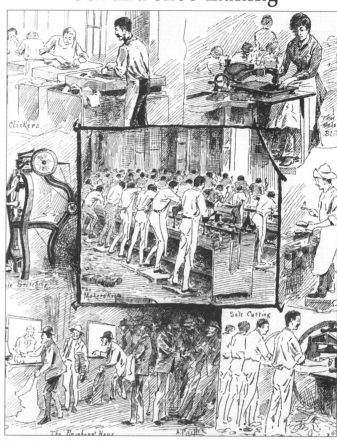

DOCUMENT 3.8

Sex and shoe-making

Opposite: *Messrs Bedggood and Co. Pty Ltd, East Melbourne. Notice the way the female workers in these photographs are described. Are similar things said about the men? Why do you think this is so? Compare the sexual division of labour in this factory in the 1930s with that in the Brisbane factory in 1889 as shown in Document 3.8.*

(*Argus*, Week-end Magazine, 6 August, 1938)

to mix either in the workshops or during meal breaks. Many employers had males and females start and finish work at different times to reduce their chances of mixing before and after work.

(See Document 3.8.)

Another reason why female boot workers were looked down on was the fact that their wages were generally lower than those in other branches of the clothing industry. This continued to be a problem well into the 1930s, when the union asked the employers to agree to a general increase in female wage rates. As the union secretary, Thomas Richards, put it to the manufacturers:

Do you think a girl can live up to the standard that generally speaking females in other industries live up to today; or do you want them to be known as 'boot trade employees', with shabby clothes, etc.?

Sewing leather uppers was also considered harder and more exacting than sewing cloth, and it was certainly dirtier. Nor were working conditions any compensation. Although some workers enjoyed the benefits of modern buildings, most had to do their work sitting on stools with no back rests. In many factories conditions were extremely primitive. Ellen Don, who began work in 1919, described the workplace at Rampling and Hall's in Collingwood, Victoria:

BEHIND THE SCENES IN INDUSTRY—No. 1

This week "The Argus" Week-end Magazine begins publication of an interesting new feature describing in pictorial form the work done in big Victorian industrial enterprises. The first of the series deals with boot and shoe manufacturing, a thriving local industry, which has practically captured the market here. These pictures were taken in the East Melbourne works of Messrs. Bedggood and Co. Pty. Ltd., the biggest manufacturers of high-grade footwear in the State. The works provide employment for 370 operatives, exclusive of office and sales staffs, and 190,000 pairs of boots and shoes are produced each year.

When a boot or shoe is made, the process begins with the fabrication of the "upper." Pieces are cut to pattern, fitted to one another, and then pulled on to lasts for proper shaping. This intricate machine pulls the uppers over the lasts.

This intent and attractive young lady is engaged on another operation in the preparation of the uppers, namely, attaching the linings (linen or leather) to the outsides, by means of a post trimming machine.

Some shoes are made inside out and turned later. That is, in the first operation, the seams are stitched on the outside and the whole shoe is pulled inside out, so that the seams finish inside. They are called "turn" or "pump" shoes, and this picture shows a section of the "turn" shoe making department.

Holes for the laces are punched and fitted with eyelets by this machine.

An exterior view of the works of Messrs. Bedggood and Co. Pty. Ltd., in East Melbourne. Next door is the original home of Victoria's first Governor, Charles Joseph La Trobe.

White shoes are sprayed with Latex rubber film to keep them clean during their passage through the factory. Here is the air-driven spray in operation.

Contentment and industrious application are expressed on the faces of these girls as they put the finishing touches to the uppers of countless shoes.

The operation is finished. Racks of completed ladies' shoes are inspected before being boxed for delivery to the retailers. And wearers of those shoes will be proud of them.

The conditions were dreadful. There was nothing hygienic whatever . . . When the bell went they all washed in a dirty little dish . . . There was no morning tea, no afternoon tea, and there was no heating system whatever. The place we were in was practically a tin shed and you could see the grass growing underneath and into the room . . . In winter time the girls used to wrap brown paper round their legs and tie it with string to keep the cold out. No sick pay or holiday pay or anything like that when I was there. The hours were from about 7.30 to 5.20 and you didn't get any smokos either, and if a girl went to the toilet and she was too long there the boss'd send you after her . . . it was a hard life. You put your head down and never raised it to knock-off time.

Pay and conditions were so bad in Melbourne's boot factories in the late 1930s, and girls so reluctant to work in them, that employers were encouraging married women to work for them by allowing them to work from nine to four (when their children would be at school).

(See Document 3.9.)

DOCUMENT 3.9

The female boot factory operative

The female operative in Australia certainly does not hold the strong position her sister does in America, though we are inclined to think her position is superior to a similar person in England. The minimum wages have just been increased to £1 per week in Victoria, and, when we consider that a girl in a Melbourne boot factory receives much higher wages than in a dressmaking or millinery establishment, and works fewer hours, it is a wonder there is [the] scarcity of girls there is at present. We have had an opportunity of seeing a good many hundreds of the boot factory girls at work, and have given particular attention to their surroundings. In every instance their surroundings were admirable. The workrooms were invariably bright, cheerful and healthy, and the girls were always clean in limb and feature, with more than a share of good looks distributed around . . .

• • • •

He led the way to a workroom on the first floor, where I saw boys and men busily engaged on the manufacture of boots; and to another on the second floor, where girls and women were similarly engaged.

The majority were undersized, small even, with a stunted appearance as though Nature had laid her scheme for them on a bolder plan than was realised; and the faces were pale from bloodlessness. Vigorous maturity . . . was wanting in the main, together with the buoyant activity and eager looks of youth, though it was present . . . And just observe the rate at which they work. No amount of vitalising energy could replace the power they are drawing off at that rate.

('Female operatives in Australia', *Australian Leather Journal* , 14 December 1907, p. 514)

(Helen Davis, 'Women who toil', *New Idea*, 6 July 1903, p. 41)

• Compare the two descriptions above. How do you explain the difference in their portrayals of female factory workers?

Food processing

Next to clothing and textile production, the most important colonial manufacturing industry which employed women was food processing. Like sewing, this was seen as a suitable occupation for women since it was the same sort of work they did in the home. Inside the factories, however, women were no longer responsible for the way in which the work was carried out. Most of the so-called skilled work was done by men, with women kept

Marchant's Hop Beer factory, Brisbane. Is there an obvious sexual division of labour in this factory? Marchant was considered a progressive man in his day. How would you describe the working conditions in his factory as portrayed in this sketch?

(*Boomerang*, 10 August 1889, p. 13)

on the more poorly paid jobs. Like the clothing trade, the work tended to be seasonal and irregular; fruit canning, for instance, was done only when the fruit was ripe, while biscuit and confectionery factories were much busier just before Christmas than during the rest of the year.

Processing huge quantities of food also caused problems for the workers which were not apparent in the average domestic kitchen. Mabel Pilling, who worked at the Mills and Ware biscuit factory in Fremantle from 1914 to 1923, recalled the problems workers had with burnt fingers:

> They'd be taking these hot biscuits off the tray and all their fingers would be bleeding because they were so tender. Their fingers were raw, red raw at the top, but you see they had to get used to that too.

Kath Stagg, who worked at the same factory in the 1930s removing biscuits from hot trays, also reported that it was very uncomfortable work:

> It was hot work running up the biscuits like that, and we were wringing wet, we had blisters on the tops of our fingers because the trays were hot.

Workers who cut and peeled fruit and vegetables also suffered from the effects of the work, the juices causing a variety of skin complaints, while women working in pickle factories had to spend their entire day on the extremely unpleasant task of onion-peeling.

Although working in tobacco factories also caused health problems for the workers (in this case the dusty atmosphere affected their lungs), they were at least relatively well paid. Mary Cain, who left a job in a boot factory because it was so hard, found much more congenial work at the Australian-British Tobacco Company in Swanston Street, Melbourne, where she worked in the stemmery:

> That was where you pulled the leaf off the stem. You'd get tobacco leaf and you had to strip it. Take the leaf off and put the stem in one bag and the leaf in a basket. And they used to take that down. We got paid by the stems. It was on piece work. We got good pay there. We got half our lodge paid and they had an insurance and housing system for their employees and they paid part of our rent. A very good firm . . .

Printing industries

Although printing and bookbinding had no direct relationship to women's domestic work, some parts of it were considered particularly appropriate for females. They were employed in large numbers to do folding and gluing, work which the Victorian Chief Inspector of Factories believed was 'admirably adapted for women, requiring as it does neatness and quick manipulation with the fingers'. However, other kinds of work which required similar skills, such as typesetting, were not considered suitable. (See Document 3.10.)

DOCUMENT 3.10

The Commonwealth Arbitration Court
and the question of female readers' assistants

The Printing and Kindred Industries Union of Australia, on its 1925 application to the Arbitration Court, asked for a prohibition on the employment of females as readers' assistants. The case arose because of reports that two girls were employed as assistants on the Adelaide Register. What follows is the exchange between Mr E. Magrath, representing the union, and the judge:

(Mr Magrath:) We submit that the work of a reader is very responsible, and his assistants should be persons on whom he could rely. The evidence of Mr Driscoll is that they are more inattentive than boys. The practice has been to have well-educated youths and adults to assist the readers, and so enable him to maintain a high standard in his work.

(His Honor:) It is not a matter of great importance, except to the girls.

People who opposed women's employment on this highly paid work argued that composing rooms were dirty and unhealthy and that women would be exposed to unsuitable literature such as anatomical texts and sensational newspapers which would harm their morals. Daily contact with males was supposed to have similarly harmful effects on a girl's timidity and modesty, while the very act of doing men's work would unsex women and make them 'manny'. The fact that female compositors in England had been seen drinking in public bars was taken as proof of this unsexing process. But the most important reason why women

(*Printing Trades Journal*, 12 January 1926, p. 45)

• What reason does the union advocate give for excluding girls from the work of assisting readers? What does this exchange reveal about the way in which women's concerns were dealt with in the Arbitration Court?

Early steam-powered paper-box making machinery which came into general use in Victoria before World War I. Note the sexual division of labour, with men performing all the 'dangerous' work on the cutting and scoring machines.

(*Town and Country Journal*, 13 April 1895, p. 30)

DOCUMENT 3.11   **Mates not enemies**

THE AUSTRALASIAN

Typographical Journal.

[REGISTERED AS A NEWSPAPER.]

MELBOURNE, JANUARY, 1890.

THE determination of Australian printers to exclude women from the composing room is neither new nor has it been arrived at without due consideration. There have been several insidious attempts to introduce what is considered by most trades unionists to be a dangerous element into the labour market. The example of New Zealand in this respect has been quoted *usque ad nauseum*, and we have no desire to play into the hands of sweaters by temporizing with this matter at all. The plain facts of the case are these :—The recent struggles which the various typographical societies have been engaged in have had the effect of bringing a large amount of non-union labour into the market. To maintain the equilibrium of labour, men have had to wander from one colony to another, very frequently with but poor success. It is the desire of every society to get employment for those men who have sacrificed everything for the cause of unionism. This can only be done by curtailing boy and abolishing girl labour. The remarks of the Queensland *Boomerang*, which are given elsewhere, are both unjust and untrue. The attitude assumed by that paper during the late trouble in Brisbane was of the most friendly character, and its views upon labour topics, as a rule, are thoroughly sound. But in its anxiety to play a chivalrous part, and espouse the cause of the fair, it is really playing into the hands of the unfair. Has there ever been an attempt to introduce female printers at a fair price? What sort of a training does the female printer get? What are the usual qualifications of a female printer? They are invariably used as the cheapest kind of labour, and are paid according to the *generosity* of their employers. They are kept at one branch of the trade—*i.e.*, "type-snatching." As to their qualification, their physical inferiority handicaps them heavily in competing against the other sex. If our contemporary needs an example of what harm can be done to a society through this evil, let him look at home. Where did the majority of the "rats" come from who are still filling the places of good men in Brisbane? The breeding cage of female labour supplied them? The question of the day is—"How shall we find employment for our men?" When that is answered, perhaps we may have time to take up the cause of the other sex. We are accused of "boycotting" women, of driving them into the nursery or kitchen. There is no foundation for the first charge. We are anxious to maintain the most friendly relations with our labouring sisters, but we are certain that the presence of women in composing rooms is not desirable, whether looked at from a moral or a hygienic point of view. We feel convinced that it will be much more to the permanent advantage of women that they should be able to cook, sew, and make their own dresses than learn a smattering of a trade which will probably be of no use to them in after life. We plead guilty to possessing what our contemporary calls "the slavish idea that one-half the race is born to cook for the other half." We simply want the "other half" to be in a position to get something to cook. Surely our Brisbane friend does not want the woman to print and the man to stop at home to make the beds ! "Because the printing trade is overflowing already, there is no reason to debar women from it." This is an extraordinary theory for a labour journal to advocate. How are wages to be maintained if a check of some sort is not brought into requisition ? The introduction into the article under review of such sentences as "the workers are plundered hand over fist by the non-producing classes," an "idle, privileged class growing up, which loafs in luxury, while the producers and distributors are finding it harder and harder to live," is to be regretted. It is hard to trace their connection with the subject under discussion, excepting upon the Mr. Dick and King Charles's head theory. The moving spirits in the "cheap and nasty" labour market are not representative master printers at all. They are either briefless barristers, decayed journalists, shady clerics, or office boys who have outgrown their stools. We are all able to face these foes to white labour, and, as a rule, beat them ; but our task is very often rendered extremely unpleasant by the introduction of a sickly sentimental herring upon our path. We are accused of selfishness, of illiberality, and sometimes of downright brutality. The fact is completely ignored that we are fighting the battle of the many and that we are honest in our intention of maintaining the dignity of labour. We read with satisfaction the scathing criticisms of the sweaters' medium, and feel that we have done our duty ; but to be called "poor-souled" by our respected contemporary is very hard to bear. However, as the actual wearer of the shoe, we have no difficulty in localizing the point of pressure ; and we must still, in self-defence, refuse to work side by side with women in the composing room. The fact has probably not been taken into consideration that some kind of apprenticeship is necessary, even for a printer. Perhaps our gallant contemporary imagines that female printers are, like critics, "ready made." Let us dispel this illusion, if it exists. The close, malodorous atmosphere of a printing office, with all its grimy surroundings, to say nothing of the abortive attempts to unravel the pothooks and hangers of the members of the "fourth estate"—these are conditions of life which permanently injure a young woman, both in body and soul. We need not point out the many paths of congenial labour which are still open to females. Dislike to domestic service is the cause of a great amount of female usefulness being diverted from its proper channel. They are not true friends to the gentle sex who advise them to enter upon overcrowded trades, necessitating standing for at least eight hours per day in a vitiated atmosphere. The humble position of a maid-of-all-work offers more scope for the proper training of a working man's wife than can be secured by taking a man's place in a printing office.

(*Australasian Typographical Journal*,
January 1890, pp. 1098–9)

• What does this exchange between William Lane and the *Australasian Typographical Journal* reveal about union attitudes to female labour? Was the printers' strategy of excluding women desirable or successful?

compositors were opposed was that they were seen to be taking men's jobs, and as such were threatening the natural order of society where men earned the money and women stayed at home and did the housework. Not all men shared this view, as the exchange between the editors of the *Boomerang* and the *Australasian Typographical Journal* shows. And some women, especially feminists, believed that women should be actively encouraged to enter such occupations to give them more employment opportunities and greater economic independence. Louisa Lawson's feminist journal, *Dawn*, deliberately recruited female compositors in the 1890s. But apart from such isolated cases, women did not set type. As in other industries which employed both sexes, women were confined to the poorly paid, so-called unskilled work. (See Documents 3.11 and 3.12.)

DOCUMENT 3.11 CONTINUED

The "Boomerang" and Female Printers.

OUR mild protest in last month's *Journal* against the employment of females in composing rooms has brought down upon us the wrath of our respected contemporary, the Brisbane *Boomerang*. He says :—

"The *Australasian Typographical Journal*, the official organ of the Australian printers' unions, comes out flat-footed against female labour, and announces an intention to 'refuse to recognize any office which employs women in the composing room.' Why? That female labour has been used to break down wages is no reason why women as women should be thus boycotted. A woman has every bit as much right to work and to live as a man has, and because the printing trade is overflowing already is no reason to debar her from it, for all trades and occupations are equally overflowing, and, anyway, her claim to admission must be considered as equal to a man's. Workmen have been so ground down themselves, have been so used as mere tools for the creation of wealth, that they often forget the place Labour should occupy, and imagine they can interfere with its due development. The woman question is a prime factor in this development. Owing to the survival of a slavish idea that half the race is born solely to cook for and bear children to the other half, women have been kept from taking part in the struggle for the readjustment of industrial conditions, and have been the millstone on the neck of Progress. Woman's mission, as the enthusiasts call it, is very different. She is a citizen of the community first and all the time, a cook and mother afterwards. She has a right to work and to the fruits of that work, equally with the best man living, and those who would continue her degradation by compelling her always to seek her livelihood as an accommodating housekeeper are simply pulling against the tide of Time. The printers won't find the girls clamouring for lower wages ; if they take them by the hand and teach them the principles of organization and the wrongs of labour they will find in women mates, not enemies ; staunch allies, not secret foes. And we are willing to guarantee this, that the first time any trade organization practically objects to women doing work which they are able to do, and for which they are paid the going wage, objecting for no other reason than that they are women, it will have against it the sympathy and support of the greater organizations of labour.

"It is a paltry thing to do, anyway, to fight the women as women—to fight any attempt to work them at a lower wage is a different thing. Here, in the world as it is now industrially constituted, the workers are plundered hand over fist by the non-producing classes. There in England, absentee dividend-drawers pose as "returned Australians." In Melbourne, in Sydney, in Brisbane, everywhere, there is an idle, privileged class growing up which loafs in luxury while the producers and distributors are finding it harder and harder to live. It is against this unjust distribution of wealth that the organization of labour and the efforts of all right-minded men are directed, not against the toiling many who ask only for leave to labour and live. One denounces the non-unionist because he weakens and undermines the fighting strength of labour unions beset by constant industrial wars, but one opens the ranks to him always, asking of him nothing more than to be a comrade and to stand by his mates as his mates will stand by him. Labour has enough to fight against without making rash war upon labourers. It fights alien races, because between the white and the coloured a great gulf is fixed, the gulf that lies betweeen civilization and conditions which for countless ages have diverged apart. But the women are of our race and of our blood, children of our common parents, mothers of our common children, speaking our tongue and thinking our thoughts, and beginning to revolt as men are beginning to revolt against the conditions which degrade and plunder men and women alike. It is at best but slight and temporary ease that the printers or any other trade or calling can gain by depriving woman of her equality, and he is a poor-souled printer who, once understanding that he can direct his energies against the conditions that crush him or against the hapless woman who is crushed with him, will not take her hand as a fellow-worker, and side by side with her fight these conditions until they are utterly overthrown and till labour is free."

DOCUMENT 3.12

A doctor reports

. . . I have come to the conclusion that much of the machinery in the Printing Trades makes very heavy demands on the girls. Its speed in many cases, not under the control of the worker, its pronounced vibration and marked jarring, and its intense specialisation with concomitant monotony are such as tend to definite nerve strain and fatigue, as well as in many instances to severe physical demands.

In the smaller factories, where there is still in existence something of the old joy of craftsmanship, because of the variety of occupation, there is no monotony, but this only covers a small percentage of the women workers in the trade. In the larger establishments there is the modern endeavour towards high output and intense specialisation, and with this comes for the individual the elimination of the joy of craftsmanship.

(Ethel E. Osborne, *Report of an Inquiry into the Conditions of Employment as Regards the Health of Female Workers in the Printing and Allied Trades*, Melbourne, 1925, p. 8)

• Dr Osborne notes several factors which determined how pleasant or stressful printing work was. What are these factors?

A female saddler at Clermont, Queensland, 1918. Although there was no mass movement of Australian women into 'men's jobs' during World War I, some women did replace enlisted men doing non-traditional work. This woman is making saddles.

(Collection, John Oxley Library, Brisbane)

Other industries

Between them, the clothing, boot, food-processing and printing industries employed about 98 per cent of all female manufacturing workers. The rest were employed in small numbers in industries such as those making matches, candles and soap, rubber goods, furniture, cosmetics, and rope. From the 1920s, there were also some women doing certain 'female' jobs in factories which made electrical and metal goods and ammunition, but by the 1930s the basic division between men's and women's work had changed very little since the gold rushes: building, construction and engineering remained as inaccessible to female labour in 1939 as in 1850, while few women did the better paid, 'skilled' work in industries where they were employed as well as men. (See Document 3.13.)

Pyrox Pty Ltd, Spark Plug factory, Abbotsford, Victoria. Manufacturing spark plugs was one of the new industries which arose in association with automobile production. Although the work performed had no traditional counterpart, a division of labour on sex lines was apparent from the outset.

(*Argus* Week-end Magazine, 25 February 1939)

DOCUMENT 3.13

'Not for my daughter'

This was the opinion expressed by a group of housewives after an inspection of a certain soap works in the city, writes one of the group to the editors.

'The lightning-like rapidity of the girls in the Sunlight soap wrapping room must seriously affect their health. Even though forced to work at such high pressure, these girls are not paid piece rates.'

'We were also amazed to find that respirators are not provided for the girls working in the department where Rinso soap powders are wrapped. The air was thick with powder, and some of the girls had scanty handkerchiefs over their mouth and nose. What an effect this must have on the lungs of these girls!'

'Over afternoon tea, provided by the firm for visitors, we all agreed this is no place for our daughters unless we want to see them become nervous wrecks.'

('Not for my daughter', *Woman Today*, August 1936, p. 19)

● What does this account suggest about the connection between high-speed work and piece rates? Can you think of other ways in which the dust problem might have been reduced besides the one adopted by these workers and that suggested by the correspondent?

Mathewson & Co., artist photographers, Brisbane. Photographers' studios provided openings for a small number of women with artistic skills in the expanding business of photographic portraiture.

(*Boomerang*, 24 August 1889)

Colonial Ammunition Company's works, Saltwater River, Victoria. The women shown in this photograph taken during the Boer War are an early example of female workers employed to make ammunition during wartime. This workplace is unusual for its time in that both sexes appear to work side by side, and both are engaged in dangerous work.

(*Leader*, Special Century Number, 1 January 1901, p. 104)

Unionism

How did female factory workers respond to their situation as poorly paid, low status employees? Many made no protest, serving their time in the factory as one would a prison sentence—dreaming of a better life in the 'happy-ever-after' of marriage. Some, like Edna Ryan's sister, Hannah, rebelled individually: they lashed out at the foremen or simply walked out and found jobs elsewhere. Others released some of their frustrations by singing songs which made fun of their bosses. Occasionally, whole workrooms erupted into screaming as one after another the workers became infected with a kind of hysteria produced by the pressures of working at speed in noisy surroundings. The managers always reacted to such outbursts by shutting down the machines, thus giving everyone a welcome break in the day's routine. But the most effective protests occurred when the workers in a whole industry joined together to present a united front to employers and to bargain for better pay and conditions.

The first recorded industry-wide strike in Australia by women occurred in 1882 when Melbourne's trouser machinists stopped work in protest against employers' attempts to cut their earnings. Mrs Ellen Cresswell, one of the strike leaders and a founder of the Victorian Tailoresses' Union, reported that this was not the first time these workers had gone on strike. She had been working as a trouser-hand in Melbourne since 1870, after being widowed ten years earlier and left with three children to support. She found that employers were always trying to cut the wages of the workers and that many of the women in individual factories had got together to try to stop this. They had failed because employers could easily sack the 'troublemakers' and get workers from other factories. The 1882–1883 strike was different. It succeeded because it was better organised, involving all the major Melbourne factories. And because it was bigger, it attracted attention from the newspapers and, through this publicity, a lot of financial support from the public. Middle-class people as well as workers wanted to help the tailoresses; they were concerned that very low rates of pay made young women vulnerable to sexual exploitation. It was a moral as much as a money issue. The cartoon of the 'sweater', although from a slightly later period, shows this common idea.

(See Documents 3.14, 3.15 and 3.16.)

Concern to protect women and children from exploitation led many colonial governments to make special laws to control the conditions in shops and factories. Not until the late 1890s, however, was any attempt made to control wages. Thereafter, special wages boards or arbitration courts (depending on which state one was in) fixed minimum rates of pay for employees in most manufacturing industries employing female labour. This encouraged workers to organise themselves into unions, because the more organised and united they were the better chance they had of getting higher minimum wages. In the twenty years before World War I a large number of women's unions were formed,

Female employees' union delegates, Brisbane, circa 1902. These female unionists were drawn mainly from the clothing trades.

(Collection, John Oxley Library, Brisbane)

DOCUMENT 3.14

The sweating evil

(Fred Booty, *Democrat*, 23 July and 6 August 1904, p.1, reproduced in Lenore Layman and Julian Goddard, *Organise!: A Visual Record of the Labour Movement in Western Australia*, Trades and Labour Council of WA, Perth, 1988, p. 119)

• What are these two cartoons saying about the causes and consequences of 'sweating'?

DOCUMENT 3.15

The workwomen's strike

Small though the strike is—merely between 200 and 300 women and girls—it has assumed a serious aspect from the fact that the girls are helpless. Men under similar circumstances can hold indignation meetings, and publicly make their grievances known; women cannot. They can only depend upon friends to champion their cause.

Lively scenes

On Thursday morning, Senator Gardiner, Acting Minister of Defence, put in an appearance, and addressed several pickets (involved in a strike by cutters at the Commonwealth Clothing Factory) . . . One of the Union officials climbed on to the sill of a window looking into the cutters' room, and appealed to the men working there to withdraw from the position they had taken up. At intervals demonstrations against the non-unionists were made by the women employed in the factory, who hooted vigorously. Matters reached a climax at the knock-off time when the unionists followed the non-unionists, and jostled and hooted them.

('The workwomen's strike', *Age*, Melbourne, 13 December 1882)

('Lively scenes', *Age*, Melbourne, 22 April 1916)

• What do these accounts of women and strikes suggest about changing ideas of accepted female behaviour between 1882 and 1916?

DOCUMENT 3.16

Remedies for sweating

2371.   How many members has the Working Women's Union? — I think there are about 400.
2372.   Are there a number of them interested in this work which is taken from the sweaters? — Yes.
2373.   Do they all take that sort of work? — Yes.
2374.   When was the union formed? — About two years ago.
2375.   I suppose they have been negotiating with the employers in endeavoring to secure a log? — Yes.
2376.   Have their efforts been crowned with any success? — Some have agreed with the log, and others would not. Those that would raise the price are cut down by the others.
2377.   There are employers who are willing to meet you? — Yes.
2378.   Do they think it is a shame that you get so little? — Yes.
2379.   It would be a good thing, I suppose, if both employers and employed in this matter were connected with some board representing both sides which would regulate the matter? — Yes.

2408.   A proposal has been made that everyone who has two women working for her should pay 10s. for registration. Would you miss 10s. taken from you in one lump? — I might miss it, but would gain it afterwards.
2409.   Do not you have to spend every penny of what you earn to live? — Yes.
2410.   If you cannot save, how could you afford to pay 10s. a year without feeling it? — Certainly we should feel it.
2411.   If the registration fee had to be paid to-morrow, would it not be inconvenient to you? — Certainly; but I would rather do it.
2412.   Why? — Because it would be better for all.
2413.   How would you get the 10s. back? — Well, it would be known who did all this work, and it would open people's eyes to what was done.
2414.   How would it raise your pay? — Well, I think some places would not be allowed to have work.
2415.   What kind of places should not have the shirts? — Well, where a husband is in full work, and has a wife and two grown up daughters, they should not be allowed to take this work and give it out to poor people to make at $3\frac{1}{2}$d. a shirt.
2416.   You think it would prevent them taking the work? — I think they should be ashamed to do it. I know people who cut out work and give it to me who would not like it known that they give out shopwork to be done. The husband is foreman of a place not far away. The daughters dress up and go out, while I have to work hard.
2417.   Apart from what might happen afterwards to benefit you, would not the mere payment of 10s. be a serious amount to one who has to work so hard as you? — Not at all. I would willingly stay up a couple of nights to earn the money.
2418.   Do you keep any books? — No. I never had a day's schooling, and could not.
2419.   Would it be a hardship if the Government compelled you to keep a book and put down what the girls earned? — I could not do it. I suppose I have children growing up who could.
2420.   Would it be an additional hardship if you had to furnish it to the inspector? — Not if the person could write.

• • • •

6059.   How long is it since you came to the conclusion that the law should interfere and say how many hours men and women should work? — If they restrict the hours of women they should treat the men in the same way.
6060.   I suppose you think it would be better for women to have votes? — Yes.
6061.   Supposing the law does not restrict men, do you think it should restrict women? — No; men should be treated the same as women.

(Evidence of Mrs Elizabeth Rogers, needlewoman, Shops and Factories Royal Commission, South Australia, 1892)

(Miss Alison McGregor, shirtmaker, Shops and Factories Royal Commission, South Australia, 1892)

• These two women were employed in the shirtmaking industry in Adelaide. From their evidence, what were they doing, or what do they think they should have been doing, to counteract low wages (or sweating) in their industry? Do you think their efforts met with success?

DOCUMENT 3.17
Policing of factory legislation

A resolution was passed by the [Women's Organising] Committee that the method of visiting the factories should be revised and condemning the practice of officers entering the workrooms separately—the inspector entering first, followed by the inspectress—sufficient opportunity thus being given to secrete work which was being carried out under conditions contravening the Factories Act; and also the non-visitation of workrooms by inspectors for two years at a time.

• • • •

It was long after I left before any improvements started in the boot trade. I suppose it'd be about five or six years after I left . . . But the inspectors came, they'd just walk in and say, 'Are you girls alright, anybody sick?', then they'd walk out with a pair of shoes under their arms.

(Labor Call, 14 July 1910)

(Collingwood History Committee, *In Those Days: Collingwood Remembered*, Carringbush Regional Library, Melbourne, 1979, p. 28)

• What do these documents suggest about the effectiveness of factory legislation in enforcing minimum standards in factories?

especially in New South Wales and Victoria, where working-class women were helped by middle-class feminists and also by male trade unionists. In the case of the male unionists, their motives for getting involved with women's unions were not always straightforward. In the printing industry, for instance, the male bookbinders were keen to amalgamate with the newly formed women's union because, as their President put it:

this [union] should endeavour to obtain some control in matters with the Women Bookbinders. Such an affiliation would strengthen our hands and the Girls could be educated as to how far they could do Bookbinding.
(See Documents 3.17 and 3.18.)

DOCUMENT 3.18
Arbitration courts and women's wages

In 1907, in his famous 'Harvester Judgement', Justice H. B. Higgins declared that the minimum adult wage should be a 'family wage', that is, sufficient for a man, his wife and their two to three children. The other side of a family wage for all men was the view that all women should receive about half the male wage:

We have no doubt that in fact she often does help her parents and her brothers and sisters; indeed it must sometimes happen that a widowed mother or an invalid husband has to be kept by the daughter or wife, or a widow has to keep her young children. Should these cases be taken into consideration? We do not think they can. They are exceptional. The normal life and career are what we have to consider. We do not lower the male living wage for bachelors or raise it for men with large families. Similarly we cannot lower it for the woman who lives at home, or raise it for the one who has to keep her husband.

(Bulletin of New South Wales Board of Trade Living Wage Adult Females 1918 Declaration, 1921, p. vi)

• Do you think it was fair to base wages on the supposedly typical male/breadwinner and female/dependant employee? Who did best out of this system? Who was worse off? Can you suggest a fairer criterion for fixing wages?

This concern to protect men's jobs caused suspicion and tension in all the major 'female' industries. Although the workers in the clothing trades did eventually unite, many men were not keen on the idea. As one of them said, 'oh let the women look after themselves, they have taken our jobs'. The food processing industry was no more united. One of the founding rules of the New South Wales Confectioners' Union in 1889 stated that 'this society discountenance all female labour in any form, in the manufacture of confectionery'. In Victoria, men and women ran separate unions until 1944.

(See Documents 3.19 and 3.20.)

Divisions between men and women in the unions hampered effective organisation of women workers in all these industries until World War II. Women's unions also faced other problems: girls and young women were often hard to unionise because they saw marriage as a more promising way of improving their lot; the seasonal lay-offs and high turnover of workers made it difficult to keep track of members; domestic responsibilities made it hard for many women to find the time for union work, while many an excellent unionist was lost to the cause through marriage. Some industries, such as clothing, were especially hard to organise because many workers worked at home, as did Eleanor early in her career. Isolated from other workers, they were virtually impossible to identify and communicate with. Some women also believed that unionism was not feminine or 'ladylike'—a problem which especially affected dressmakers and milliners. As one

The Denton Hat Mills, Victoria. Both men and women engaged in making felt hats were among the most successful clothing trade unionists, which was reflected in their wages and conditions. What evidence is there in this photograph that conditions in felt hat factories were better than those in the clothing trades generally, as described in the text?

(*Leader*, Special Century Number, 1 January 1901, p. 103)

DOCUMENT 3.19

Reminiscences of a militant woman

I recall . . . It would be 1915 or 16. Not too many women active in political and industrial circles in those days—and it prompted the question as to why I was not enjoying myself at less serious gatherings than Trades Hall activities. I was told I should be thinking of being a wife *and* mother. I said I had no intention of being either. To me it was more important to work for a better system of society than to bring more children into a world to be exploited by the employing class. This was met by one of this group of men that it was wrong to leave the breeding and care of the next generation to those who were not intelligent.

(Notes by May Brodney on W. B. Scott, Ms 10882 Brodney Papers, La Trobe Collection, State Library of Victoria)

- What do these opinions on women's 'proper sphere' expressed by working men, have in common with those expressed by men in Document 1.6, 'The sex of labour'? (See Chapter 1, p. 9). How do you think women such as May Brodney coped in a largely male world which did not welcome their presence?

DOCUMENT 3.20

Unionists victimised
At Hoadley's Chocolates Limited
Girl Victimised for Joining Union
The Union Officials Responsible, Melbourne

About January, 1932, one of the girls employed by Hoadley's was able to induce eight or nine others to join the Union. The news of their action arrived back at the factory before the girls, and it is assumed that the Union officials acquainted Walter Hoadley of the fact that the girls were joining the Union. This led to the dismissal of the girl, and the others were told to go outside and reconsider their decision. Eventually, W. Hoadley went out to them and told them if they had decided to 'dump' the Union they could remain, which they did.

Although the employees of this firm are not allowed to join the Union, they must buy a ticket for the Union picnic or lose one day's pay, [under the Wage Board award] but on the other hand were not allowed time off to attend the picnic, or they would lose their jobs.

The average wage of the girls is: Piecework, 2/6 to 3/6 per day. Occasionally they are permitted to earn up to 7/- per day, but this is seldom.

Another action of the firm that the girls complain bitterly of, is that they have to submit to be searched for a few chocolates that the boss suspects have taken their fancy. They are almost stripped and the searchers, who are women, run their hands over them, all the time making the most insulting gestures, to indicate that they might become contaminated with such close contact with the girls.

('At Hoadley's Chocolates Limited: girl victimised for joining union', *Working Woman*, September 1932, p. 3, La Trobe Collection)

- What problems does this account suggest there were for female unionists at Hoadley's chocolate factory?

DOCUMENT 3.21

The union and the Lucas company

Ballarat Trades Council: letter received as to forming a branch of the whiteworkers. It was decided that Mr Cain go to Ballarat and organise the workers and inaugurate a Branch.

• • • •

Messrs Smith and Keane, representing the Federated Clothing Trades Union, yesterday interviewed Mr Price, manager of Lucas' Clothing Factory. Mr Price told the union officials that he disapproved of unionism and would be very displeased if any of his 450 girls joined the union. When asked what he would do about those employees who displeased him, he said they would be the first to go in slack time.

• • • •

When Mr Edward Price, manager of Lucas' Clothing Company, yesterday visited the factory workrooms he was given a rousing reception by the employees, the machines being turned off and the girls singing 'For He's a Jolly Good Fellow'. Mr Price thanked the girls for their support and added:

'Now a word in regard to the new rates and wages. Those who are now receiving more than the minimum will also receive more than the new minimum, and we hope, with the study of the principles of efficiency, without the necessity of working any harder, that you will find it just as possible, under the new rate of wages, to make as large a bonus as before. There are many ways in which the principles of efficiency can be studied and carried out.'

Mr Price again thanked the girls for their loyalty, to which the girls responded with a hearty cheer, and work was resumed as usual.

• • • •

The great triumph for the principles of unionism gained in the controversy between the Trades and Labour Council and the firm of Lucas and Company, was referred to last night, at the usual meeting of the Trades and Labour Council. Mr A. Rowe presided, and when the meeting opened Mr E. A. Smith introduced a large number of young ladies who had joined the union. They were received with loud applause and given seats in the gallery.

(Minutes of Federated Clothing Trades Union, Victorian Branch (No. 2 Group), 17 April 1917, ANU Archives)

(*Ballarat Star*, May 1917)

(*Ballarat Star*, July 1917)

(*Ballarat Star*, July 1917)

• What do the above extracts from union minutes and the local newspaper tell us about relations between the employers, workers and union officials at the Lucas clothing company?

unionist complained, too many of her workmates thought that 'by joining a union you were lowering yourself'. The Victorian Female Confectioners' Union struck a similar attitude, and countered it with a positive assertion of the value of 'womanliness' rather than 'ladylike' behaviour. Its journal, the *Woman's Clarion*, proclaimed:

> Give us that grand old word 'Woman'
> And let's have done with 'Lady'.

DOCUMENT 3.22

The strikers

A girl, only breadwinner for a family of five. She was a leader of her group in the strike. Her young man came down from the bush to marry her, she refused because she could not afford to leave her family destitute. She also was the last girl to return to work, because some of them were not put on immediately.

● ● ● ●

A widow woman, with five children all going to school, trying to educate the eldest, a very smart boy. She was a militant strike leader and said it was worth the sacrifice to get the task rates and respect which they deserved from their employers.

● ● ● ●

A girl, only breadwinner for a family of seven, being in ill-health herself said that the sacrifice would be great, but would be with the men and girls in their protest against wages reductions and sweating.

● ● ● ●

Girls picketing at a certain factory were surrounded, outside the factory, by police and plain-clothes detectives, but were undeterred by this show of authority, [and] stood their ground, in spite of the strong arm of the law.

(Notes made by Clothing Trades Union official on some of the participants and incidents in the 1935 strike of trouser machinists in Melbourne, University of Melbourne Archives)

● What do these notes say about the motives of female clothing workers who went on strike in 1935?

For other women, unions were not an option. They existed on the margins of the work-force, living from hand to mouth. Their plight is the subject of Chapter 4.
(See Documents 3.21 and 3.22.)

Notes

Louisa O'Neil—Taped interview by Kay Hopwood, Melbourne University Archives, 1984.

Edna Ryan—*Two-Thirds of a Man: Women and Arbitration in New South Wales 1902–1908*, Hale & Iremonger, Sydney, 1984, pp. 12–13.

Lesbia Harford—D. Modjeska and M. Pizer (eds), *The Poems of Lesbia Harford*, Angus & Robertson, North Ryde, 1985.

'A woman'—Helen Davis, 'The women who toil', *New Idea*, 6 July 1903.

Justice H. B. Higgins—Judgement in Federated Clothing Trades Union of Australia vs Archer *et al.*, 1919, p. 14, ANU Archives of Business and Labour, E138/18/8.

Ruth Haynes—Collingwood History Committee, *In Those Days: Collingwood Remembered*, Carringbush Regional Library, Melbourne, 1979.

Dorothy White—Taped interview by Kay Hopwood, Melbourne University Archives, 1984.

Gertrude Flynn—Transcript of Evidence to 1927 Commonwealth Arbitration Court Hearing, Clothing Trades Case, p.2375, ANU Archives of Business and Labour, E/138/18/26.

Thomas Richards—Minutes, 1935 Interstate Conference, p. 18, Australian Boot Trade Employees Federation Deposit, ANU Archives of Business and Labour, T5/3/2.

Ellen Don—Collingwood History Committee, *op. cit.*, p. 27.

Mabel Pilling—Jan Carter, *Nothing to Spare: Recollections of Australian Pioneering Women*, Penguin, Ringwood, 1986, p. 80.

Kath Stagg—Shirley Booth, 'Burnt Fingers: Mills & Ware Biscuits 1898–1952', in R. Frances and B. Scates (eds), *The Murdoch Ethos: Essays in Honour of Foundation Professor Geoffrey Bolton*, Murdoch University, WA, 1989, p. 81.

Mary Cain—Collingwood History Committee, *op. cit.*, p. 29.

Victorian Chief Inspector of Factories—Report Chief Inspector of Factories, Victoria, 1886, p. 6.

'timidity and modesty' etc.—*Australasian Typographical Journal*, 1 June 1906, p. 11.

Dawn—J. Hagan, 'An incident at the *Dawn*', *Labour History*, No.8, May 1965, pp. 19–20; B. Matthews, 'Dawn Crusade; Louisa Lawson', in Eric Frey (ed.), *Rebels and Radicals*, George Allen & Unwin, Sydney, 1983, pp. 148–62.

Ellen Cresswell—R. Frances, 'The politics of work: case studies of three Victorian industries, 1880–1939', PhD thesis, Monash University, 1988, pp. 102–4.

President of male bookbinders union—Victorian Bookbinders and Paper Rulers Union, Minutes, 23 April 1912. Manuscript at Printing and Kindred Industries Employees Union, Melbourne.

'oh let the women look after themselves . . .'—Quoted by Herbert Carter, Commonwealth Court of Conciliation and Arbitration, Amalgamated Clothing Trades Union of Australia vs Alley *et al.*, Transcript of Evidence, p. 22, ANU Archives of Business and Labour, #138/118/86.

'by joining a union you were lowering yourself'—Julia Northausen, *Australian Clothing Trades Journal*, Merrifield Collection, Melbourne.

Role-play—Based on 'Committee of Inquiry into Conditions of Female Labour of H. V. McKay Pty Ltd', 1927, Melbourne University Archives, and R. Frances, 'H. V. McKay: man and myth', unpublished 3RRR *History Show* script, 1984.

SUGGESTIONS FOR STUDY

For discussion

1 If you had been a clothing trade worker, what sort of clothes would you have wanted to make?

2 Which kind of clothing manufacture provided the best conditions? the worst?

3 What sort of women and girls worked in the boot factories? Were they of a different class to clothing workers?

4 You will have noticed that clothing and shoe shops have different stock depending on the weather or season. When do you think the workers who made clothing/shoes would be busiest? When would they be least busy?

5 Were the busy seasons in clothes and boot factories the same as those in the food processing industry?

6 The ideology of femininity affected the types of industrial work women did. Discuss the different ways ideas about suitable women's work influenced female employment in each of the industries described. Have these ideas changed?

7 Were men and women unionists fighting for the same things?

8 Why would some employers and other middle-class people support better wages and conditions for female workers?

To write about

1 Write a poem describing the experience of working in a factory of your choice in the nineteenth century, for example, a pickle factory, a boot factory, or a firm that makes stationery.

2 Read Edward Bartlett's evidence to the Royal Commission (Document 3.4). Think about how the women who worked for him would have felt. Write a transcript of the evidence that one of his workers might have given to the same Commission.

3 Imagine you are a factory inspector. Your niece in England is thinking of emigrating to Australia and has asked you to advise her about the different kinds of factory employment available for girls (she is sixteen years old). Write a reply to her letter explaining her options and the advantages and disadvantages of various types of work. Don't forget to date your letter.

4 Read the column in the *Australasian Typographical Journal* (Document 3.11) opposing women's entry into the trade. Imagine you are a female compositor working at *Dawn*. Write a reply.

Community resources

Labour and industry

1 Visit a nearby factory. How is the factory floor organised and does it segregate male from female labour? Is the organisation of work different from the late nineteenth century?

2 Describe the working environment of your chosen factory. Note the speed and stress of work, hazards and the noise of machinery. What protective clothing is provided and what measures are taken to reduce the monotony of the work? When were these measures introduced and who instigated them?

3 Interview any of the female workers employed in the factory. Did their mothers also work there? How have conditions changed in the industry? Can any of these women realistically aspire to management positions?

4 Invite a spokesperson for the union movement into your classroom. Ask her or him about the achievements of unions and the difficulties of organising female labour. Has unionism achieved as much for female as for male workers? Do their needs differ?

5 Role-play

Set up a role-play with the following characters and guidelines:

Scene: Committee of Inquiry into the employment of female labour at H. V. McKay's Sunshine Harvester works, Braybrook, Victoria.

Year: 1927.

Location: Melbourne, Victoria.

Characters:

The Commissioners conducting the inquiry:

• Miss Muriel Heagney, feminist and labour activist, nominated by the Trades Hall Council. She is an advocate of women's right to work and of equal pay for the sexes.

- Dr Ethel Osborne, medical practitioner who has conducted numerous inquiries into the health of female workers, nominated by the Victorian Department of Labour. She is very concerned about the effects of modern repetitive methods of production on workers.
- Dr Kate McKay, medical practitioner employed by the Victorian Department of Labour to monitor the health of women in industry. She has been nominated by H. V. McKay Pty Ltd. She is very concerned that industrial work might have bad effects on women's future roles as mothers.

The witnesses:

- Mr Ralph McKay, son of H. V. McKay (the owner) and manager of H. V. McKay's bolt and core department (where the 'girls' are employed). Acutely aware of the cost-savings involved in employing young female workers, he is anxious to portray the work as suitably 'feminine', but is evasive about female rates of pay.
- Mr Henderson, secretary of the Ironmoulders Union. Although his main concern is to protect the jobs of his members against the competition of female labour, he is shrewd enough to see that such arguments might not convince the three women on the committee. He emphasises the moral and health risks of such work for women.

    As the Union's representatives have been forbidden access to the workshops by the management, this man's evidence is based on reports from union members at the McKay factory and observations of conditions in other engineering firms.

- 'Miss Mary Smith', aged seventeen, is employed to feed bolts into a pointing machine. Her father is also employed at the works. The eldest of eight children, she hands all her earnings to her mother and helps with housework after leaving the factory. She prefers engineering work to her previous job in a dusty pottery works.
- 'Miss Jane Brown', aged thirty, is employed as a fitter. She began work at the McKay factory in 1915 (during World War I) as one of the few women employed on engineering work. She was put off at the end of the war (1918). Her fiancé was killed in action in France so she

remained single. Lives with and partially supports her widowed mother.

- 'Mr John Smith', father of Mary Smith, also works at the McKay factory. He heard of the vacancy in the bolt section and told his daughter to apply. He likes to have her in the same factory and sees nothing unsuitable in the work.

Situation:

Ever since its beginnings in Ballarat in the 1880s, H. V. McKay's agricultural machinery manufacturing business has been beset by industrial conflict. H. V. McKay is a fiercely independent and tough man, strongly opposed to unions and arbitration of any kind. His firm seizes every opportunity to undermine the influence of the union at the factory (which moved to the outskirts of Melbourne in 1904). In 1925 the company introduces female labour into its bolt and core-making section, arguing that females are more productive workers and are more suitable than boys in monotonous, repetitious, 'dead-end' jobs. There is an outcry from the male workers, who see these female workers as a threat to the jobs of male breadwinners and to the status and livelihood of skilled tradesmen. They protest through the union to the Victorian Department of Labour. This department shares the concern widely expressed during the inter-war years that paid work is harmful to women's health and especially bad for their reproductive capacities.

The committee of inquiry is appointed and instructed to inquire into:

a Whether the employment of females in such industries is likely to be injurious to the health of workers;

b Whether there is any other sufficient reason, apart from the effect of the work done on the health of the workers, why females should not be employed in such industries.

The scene opens with the committee hearing evidence from the union secretary, who is explaining why he believes women should not be employed at the Sunshine Harvester works.

4 On the Margins

Aboriginal women

Whatever hardships Eleanor may have suffered one fact was always in her favour: she was white. The invasion and occupation of their land left Aboriginal people with little choice other than to work on the fringes of the white economy. As hunting grounds gave way to crops, sheep and cattle, many Aboriginal people drifted from the country to the city; disease, government policy and missionary activity broke up tribes and families.

In the early 1920s, one Nyungar girl found herself in Perth, several hundred miles from the land of her ancestors. She and her family lived in shanties on the Swanbourne foreshore, sheltering from the wind and heat in humpies of tin and canvas. During summer the family often found seasonal work, mostly on the farms located on the outskirts of the city. But during winter, Aboriginal people survived off a meagre government ration of tea, salt and sugar and whatever else they could earn. This Nyungar girl, like many others, went scrubbing and cleaning, returning to camp each day with a penny or two and whatever food she could scavenge. She was lucky. Despite poverty, disease and discomfort, the camp kept alive a sense of community crucial to Aboriginal identity. The old stories could still be told, the songs sung and kinsfolk could keep close to one another. But many Aboriginal women who went to work in the city were forced to leave their homes far behind them. From the 1880s to the 1930s, girls as young as thirteen were taken to Melbourne from the distant Lake Tyers mission. There they were put to work as domestic servants, at wages even less than girls like Eleanor received. Most Aboriginal domestics received a shilling a week 'pocket money', scarcely enough to supplement their meagre rations. The remainder of the three shilling wage was paid into a 'trust' account administered by the Aboriginal Protection Board and the girls' employers. Often these entrusted wages proved a disappointment to their owners, the amount whittled away by fines arbitrarily imposed by employers or misappropriated by public servants.

(See Document 4.1.)

DOCUMENT 4.1

Protection or persecution

Aborigines Protection Board: Ward Register

19 August, 1916

Name: Dodds, Lily, H. C.   *Age*: 13 years

Place of Birth: Walgett   *Religion*: Church of England

Reasons for Board assuming control of Child: Orphan

Father's name, occupation and address: Unknown

Mother's name and address: Deceased

To Which Home Sent: Cootamundra, 6 Oct 1916

Disposal: Left Cootamundra Home 20/4/17. Sent to Mrs. Harper, Croyden, returned 26/4/17. Sent to Mrs Broughton, Maidment St, Cremorne, returned 3/5/17 and sent to Mrs. Cook, Wentworth Rd, Vaucluse. Absconded 27/3/20. Found by Police and committed to Central Police Station, to Tempe Convent next day.

Entered employment of Mrs. Whittall, 'Sherwood Lange', Smithfield 11/11/20. Absconded 18/2/22 and returned Tempe Convent. Absconded and sent to Salvation Army Home, Stanmore. Transferred to Mrs. L. C. Carole, 'Hillview', Trewilga 8/8/22. Absconded and entered service of Mrs. Arthur Stanford, Lynda Vale, Peak Hill, 20/2/23. Absconded 10/3/24.

Again absconded and returned to her people. Said to be married to a man named Cunningham at Peak Hill.

(Aborigines Welfare Board of New South Wales, Ward Register, Nos. 1–500, Archives Office of New South Wales, reproduced in Megan McMurchy, Margaret Oliver and Jeni Thornley, *For Love or Money*, Penguin, Ringwood, 1989, p. 94)

• Why did the Board 'assume control' of Lily Dodds? What kind of controls could the Board exercise over her life?
• What did Lily learn at the Cootamundra Home? What does this suggest about employment prospects for Aboriginal women at this time?
• Why did Lily 'abscond' from her employers?

The work performed by these servants was demanding and demeaning. They scrubbed the clothes and floors of white mistresses, mistresses who invariably called them European names such as 'Mary' or 'Anne'. A majority of girls from Lake Tyers lasted only a few years in service, returning home to give birth to 'half-caste' babies. Often their babies were taken from them. Government policy for much of this period favoured the assimilation of Aborigines into white society. 'Full-bloods' were to be isolated on reserves where their old way of life would die with them. 'Half-castes' were to be introduced to the 'civilising' effects of white society; their 'white blood' (it was thought) would make them more receptive to white ways. One such girl was Daisy Corunna.

Daisy grew up on Corunna Downs Station in Western Australia. Her mother was a housemaid for Howden Drake-Brockman, a wealthy pastoralist and owner of the station. The identity of her father was never legally established: but Daisy was certain it was her mother's master. Whoever her father was, Daisy was a half-caste 'too black for the whites and too white for the

blacks . . . stuck in the middle'. At fourteen she was taken from her crying mother's arms and sent 'to schooling' in the city, so her employers told her. Daisy was really destined to a life of service in the Drake-Brockmans' mansion. Work and sleep were all she could find time for.

Aboriginal girls in training for domestic service, Cootamundra Girls' Home, NSW, 1820–1930. Children like these were frequently taken from their families to serve in white households.

(Aboriginal Welfare Board, Archives Office of NSW)

Aboriginal Camp, Lake Monger, Leederville, Perth, late 1920s. Urban Aboriginal people lived on the fringes of the white economy in more than one sense.

(Battye Library, 2450B)

By jingoes, washing was hard work in those days. The old laundry was about twenty yards from the house and the troughs were always filled with dirty washing. They'd throw everything down from the balcony onto the grass, I'd collect it up, take it to the laundry and wash it. Sometimes, I thought I'd never finish stokin' up that copper, washin' this and washin' that. Course, everything was starched in those days. Sheets, pillowcases, serviettes, tablecloths, they was all starched. I even had to iron the sheets. Isn't that silly, you only goin' to lay on them.

The house had to be spotless. I scrubbed, dusted and polished. There was the floors, the staircase, the ballroom. It all had to be done.

Soon, I was the cook too. Mind you, I was a good cook. I didn't cook no rubbish. Aah, white people, they got some funny tastes. Fussy, fussy, aaah, they fussy. I 'member I had to serve the toast on a silver tray. I had to crush the edges of each triangle with a knife. Course, you never left the crusts on sandwiches, that was bad manners. Funny, isn't it? I mean, it's all bread, after all.

I had my dinner in the kitchen. I never ate with the family. When they rang the bell, I knew they wanted me. After dinner, I'd clear up, wash up, dry up and put it all away. Then, next morning, it'd start all over again. You see, it's no use them sayin' I was one of the family, 'cause I wasn't. I was their servant.

Like her mother before her, Daisy Corunna fell pregnant out of wedlock. Her child's parentage (like her own) was never legally established, but many believe Gladys was fathered by the same Drake-Brockman who it is believed fathered Daisy twenty years earlier. Mother and child were quickly separated. Gladys was sent to learn domestic service at the Parkerville Children's Home; Daisy returned to her chores at the Drake-Brockman mansion. The two saw each other briefly over the Christmas holidays, and then only when it suited the Drake-Brockmans' arrangements. Life at the orphanage was far from easy. The girls were woken early each morning, they swept the floors and made the beds before a frugal breakfast of bread and dripping, and weevil-infested porridge. The day's routine seldom varied. Aboriginal girls spent their time scrubbing, sewing and cooking; only the white girls were able to do lessons as well as their 'domestic' work. Most of their tasks were tiring and monotonous, designed to instil the 'virtues' of discipline and obedience. But girls like Gladys took every chance they could to escape the institution. Often they went for walks through the bush, foraging for berries or swimming in the river and their loneliness was made a little easier by the friendships which bound their lives together. Gladys was eleven years old when she and her mother were reunited. By then she had learnt to deny her Aboriginality, and later married a white man in the hope of financial security and social acceptance. When Gladys's child Sally was born in 1951 her Aboriginal identity was hidden from her: Sally (now Sally Morgan) grew up believing there was 'a touch of Indian' in the family. The search for her real identity provided much of the impetus for Sally Morgan's successful career as an artist and writer.

White women in poverty

It was not only black women who were poor and isolated in Australia's towns and cities. Poor white women, like black women, lived on the margins of white society: often despised, despairing and dependent on welfare or charity.

Among the workless, feeding the hungry. 'The deserving poor': approved applicants queue for meals during the 1890s depression. Who are the recipients of charity in this picture?

(*Illustrated Australian News*, 1 July 1892)

Distributing food at the South Melbourne Depot.

(*Leader*, 14 April 1894)

As the 1890s depression deepened, conventional lines of relief broke down. Compare these two scenes, two years apart.

As Eleanor's life has shown, women were particularly susceptible to poverty. When their husbands died or deserted, women were left alone to care for the young and the elderly. It was their meagre earnings which tipped the scales away from destitution. Their work was always on the fringes of the paid economy. Women took in sewing or washing or went out cooking and cleaning. But often the work they found was not enough to sustain them. In times of depression, both in the 1890s and 1930s, middle-class families made do without the services of a maid or a cleaner. Both women and men walked from suburb to suburb pleading for work. Scavenging became a necessity for survival. Families squatted in abandoned houses and scoured rubbish bins for food and clothing. And as the national economy moved from bad to worse, women created an economy of their own to replace it, bartering goods with neighbours, exchanging food for services, tending chooks and gardens in backyards and pawning whatever was left of their possessions. When all these options were exhausted destitute families turned to charity for their survival. Eleanor had been fortunate in that her difficult time had coincided with a boom in the economy: people gave freely to help her, mindful that their willingness to give was a measure of moral worth. And Eleanor herself was 'deserving'. Her predicament was caused through her husband's death, not by any individual failing. She was honest and hardworking, shunned drink and attended church. Giving to Eleanor would be a way of rewarding her example.

(See Document 4.2.)

The family of a dying man pose for Benevolent Society photographer, 1891. The loss of a male breadwinner was devastating for any working-class family.

(Benevolent Society, *A Merry Christmas to the Poor*, Sydney, 1891)

DOCUMENT 4.2

Life on the margins

Visitors' reports on Mrs Denny

7 July 1895 Bros. Willow and Fitzgerald visited. She expects to be put out on the street on Monday. She heard that her husband is working in a brewery in Kew, Victoria. Brother Cassidy has friends there and he is suggested to write and make inquiries.

14 July 1895 Bros. Sherord and Wesley visited. She is unable to pay the rent and has been put out on the street. Removed to No. 60 Henson Street. Unable to pay rent.

25 August 1895 Bros. Bourke and Kennedy visited. She received a telegram from her husband saying that he was very badly burned and in hospital. Borrowed 3/- to reply to message. Case remains same.

13 October 1896 Visited by Bros. Fitzgerald and Cameron but she was out on Saturday evening. He and Bourke visited. She said she would rather do without order than have her things inquired into but afterwards pleaded ignorance of the duties of the Brothers and promised it would not happen again. Decided to give 2/- for rent.

17 November 1895 Visited by Bros. Bourke and Fitzgerald. She is still in the same position. The President heard from Mrs Clark that she does not pay the rent regularly. Bros. Seymour and Wesley . . . are to make inquiries about this.

15 December 1895 Brother Seymour visited twice. She has had no word from her husband. She is in arrears for rent and the landlord threatens to turn her out.

29 December 1895 Brother Seymour visited. She has had no word from husband since landlady gave her notice to leave the house. She has told the President that she did not intend to pay the rent so on this account he did not give her the Christmas order. The Vice-President said he was pleased with Brother Seymour's actions.

26 January 1896 The President visited. The nuisance inspector visited her house during the week but when she explained her case they decided not to prosecute her. Mr Conlon informed Brother Cassidy that he sent for her the other day to do some work but she would not come. Same grant.

2 February 1896 Brother Seymour visited twice. She said her husband had sufficiently recovered to enable him to leave hospital. Some woman placed her case in the *Sunday Times* to try and get assistance for her. Same order, 2 shillings.

1 March 1896 No news from the husband. She received the sum of £2 6s. from the *Sunday Times*.

12 April 1896 She now intends issuing a warrant for her husband's arrest. She earnt a few shillings at Conlon's.

(Extracted from the Minutes of the St Vincent de Paul Society, St Bede's Branch, Pyrmont, July 1895–March 1896, Mitchell Library, Sydney, ML MS 2984 K15516.

• How did Mrs Denny support herself when her husband went looking for employment? What do these extracts suggest about her relationship with charity? Would Mrs Denny's situation improve after the arrest of her husband?

*'Old woman sitting in doorway,
circa 1900'. Advancing years meant
an increasing struggle for survival
rather than retirement for members
of the working class. Before the
introduction of old age pensions in
1908, such women were often forced
to take shelter in 'benevolent
asylums'.*

(Archives Office of NSW)

Less fortunate women felt the want of charity. Throughout the 1890s and 1930s, thousands of families became dependent entirely on its meagre assistance. Governments made little provision for them. Women were not eligible for the dole in the Great Depression, even if their husbands had deserted them. Nor could they find work on relief projects; clearing scrub and building roads was not considered suitable work for a woman. The situation in the 1890s depression had been even more difficult. In the days before the dole, the welfare of women and men alike was left entirely at the discretion of charities. In Eleanor's day an energetic church or ladies committee could generally raise enough funds to get by: a cake stall, a bazaar and private donations were enough to buy Eleanor her small cottage in James Street. But in times of depression the rich were no longer willing to give and the poor

Unemployment and evictions forced many families to take to the road in search of substistence. Why do you think the man on the right is in uniform?

(*Labour Daily*, circa 1931, in M. McMurchy, M. Oliver and J. Thornley, *For Love or Money: A Pictorial History of Women and Work in Australia*, Penguin, Ringwood, 1983, p. 99)

Noel Counihan's, At the start of the march, 1932. *Unable to feed their children, men and women demonstrated in the streets during the 1930s depression. Their protests sometimes succeeded in extracting concessions from governments which improved the plight of the unemployed.*

(Painting by Noel Counihan (1913–1986). Copyright Pat Counihan. Art Gallery of NSW)

were multiplied a hundred times over. By the 1890s, charities doled out a single loaf of bread for each of their many applicants; most charities were unable to make provision for rent, clothes, shoes or medicine. And in granting aid, charities became more and more discriminating. Philanthropic women called upon the poor not just to offer advice and comfort, but also to assess their eligibility for assistance. Women were denied relief on the grounds that they were 'dirty and disreputable', and 'thriftless, brawling or noisy'. One widow had her assistance cut off following complaints from her landlady that she had 'been out at night' and 'come home bringing a disreputable looking man with her'. Claims of drinking, improvidence and other failings of character could also jeopardise assistance, even if based on dubious sources.

(See Document 4.3.)

DOCUMENT 4.3

Deserving and undeserving
Charity Organisation Society. Case Histories

Cases described as 'satisfactory'

Cause of distress: exceptional misfortune

A widow, advanced in years; respectable and deserving, with a family to maintain. Home broken up. Was induced by a friend to come to Melbourne to earn her living. Very shortly after left to her own resources by said friend. Recommended for employment.

Cause of distress : illness

An old woman, deserving and respectable. Had a little home, and supported herself by charring. Met with an accident which incapacitated her from working. Old employer found, willing to befriend her.

Cause of distress: insufficient demand for services

A single young lady, aged 30. Profession, governess and teacher. Assisted out here by an Emigration Society. Character, good: desire for and ability to work satisfactorily proved. Three months here, and had only obtained partial employment—neither permanent nor sufficiently remunerated. Loan obtained for her, which, some little time afterwards, having obtained suitable employment, she honourably repaid.

Case described as 'doubtful'

Cause of doubt: desire to dictate form of assistance

A young married woman, unable to agree with husband; he deserted her; she obtained order for maintenance; had him arrested and imprisoned for failure to obey order. Wanted the Society to obtain material and tools to enable her to work at a trade at which she said she was proficient. Request granted, and amount she mentioned provided. When she found that *materials* and not *money* were to be given, she declined assistance altogether. She said she 'wouldn't be treated like a pauper'.

Cases described as 'unsatisfactory'

Cause of doubt: begging-letter imposters

A married 'lady' wrote to a very prominent Government official, describing herself as perfectly destitute and penniless. Inquiry showed that she was a very improvident woman, living in a style beyond her means, and undertaking responsibilities in a reckless fashion. Her husband was earning £9 per month and his 'keep'.

Cause of doubt: imposing on public institutions

A young married woman of 21, admitted 'free' to the Women's Hospital. The family owns ten acres of garden-land (very valuable) near Melbourne. Other facts to prove that she had no claim for public gratuitous treatment. Authorities recommended to enforce payment.

(Charity Organisation Society, Victoria, *Annual Report*, 1889, appendix)

• What do these extracts reveal about the causes of women's poverty in late nineteenth century Australia? How did women such as these survive?

• How did the Charity Organisation Society distinguish between its deserving and undeserving applicants? On what terms would it grant relief and what form did that relief take?

• Why was the case of 'a young married woman, unable to agree with her husband' refused relief? What does her response tell us about the experience of poverty?

• Why was 'a young married woman of 21' prosecuted by the authorities? Did she (in your opinion) have a claim to 'gratuitous treatment'?

Clarinna Stringer was a typical example of a woman living on the margins. Her husband's death left her to care alone for five children. Unable to earn a wage elsewhere, the family set up a wood-yard, managing the makeshift business from the back of their Carlton home. But even Clarinna's resourcefulness could not ward off the effects of the 1890s depression; by 1892, the Victorian economy had all but collapsed and even in the coldest weather customers made do without a winter fire. Charity refused to help her; on two occasions she applied for relief from the Ladies Benevolent Society and both times her application was rejected. Clarinna Stringer was one of the doubtful cases. The youngest children should have been at school, not at work in the wood-yard; the eldest might be better placed elsewhere. Moreover, as a woman on her own, Clarinna would have been considered morally suspect. Earning a living was of course admirable, but not in the view of nineteenth-century society, if it was an attempt at personal independence. By June, Clarinna was unable to pay her 15 shillings rent; the bailiffs moved in to evict the family and confiscate what little she had left.

What makes Clarinna's story so interesting is her defiance. Unable to beat off the bailiffs alone, she called on the community to help her. The residents of Tyne Street turned out in force, some three hundred people loading furniture, bedding and even the stock in the wood-yard into a cart and wheeling it away. For several hours Clarinna's possessions were at the centre of a conflict between landlords and tenants, the people and the police. First the goods were recaptured by the authorities and impounded at a local auctioneer's premises. Then the mob regrouped, tearing up the newly tarred road and hurling hunks of blue metal at the window of the store. The riot ended as the owner fired his rifle into the crowd and mounted police charged, batons drawn, at his assailants.

When the dust finally settled it was clear Clarinna (and her sympathisers) had been defeated. She had lost her home, her possessions and most important of all the means of earning a livelihood. It may not have been much but the wood-yard was the symbol and means of Clarinna's independence. Without it she was left to the mercy of the charities and the police. Like so many women of this period, Clarinna disappeared from history, her story lost in the anonymity poverty often brings. But the same story was to be re-enacted forty years later, as the unemployed and their families banded together to resist eviction or pooled their resources to make ends meet.

(See Document 4.4.)

Charity directory

Alfred Hospital	Mr. R. L. J. Ellery
Austin Hospital for Incurables	Mr. T. Harlin
Australian Church Social Improvement Soc.	*Mrs. Dickson*
Benevolent Asylum	Mr. C. Cock
Brighton Ladies' Benevolent Society	Mrs. A'Beckett
Brunswick Relief Society	Mrs. George
Caledonian Society	
Carlton Refuge	Mrs. Sugden and Mrs. W. S. Puckle
Convalescent Home for Women	Mrs. Pennington
Convalescents' Aid Society for Men	Colonel Goldstein
Discharged Prisoners' Aid Society	Mr. E. L. Zox, M.L.A.
Elizabeth Fry Retreat	Mr. J. Swinburn
Friendly Brothers' Society, Richmond	Rev. Jas. Kennedy
Homœopathic Hospital	Mr. C. Hudson
Immigrants' Aid Society's Home	Mr. Wm. Hartnell
Jewish Philanthropic Society	Mr. W. B. Isaacs
Melbourne Hospital	Mr. John Grice
Melbourne District Nursing Society	Rev. M. M. Whitton
Melbourne Hospital for Sick Children	
Melbourne Jewish Aid Society	Mr. P. Blashki
Melbourne Ladies' Benevolent Society	Mrs. Jamieson
Melbourne Orphan Asylum	Mr. Edwin Exon
Prahran, South Yarra, and Toorak Ladies' Benevolent Society	Mrs. Clendinning
Prison Gate Brigade & Rescued Sisters' Home	Commissioner Coombes
Richmond Dispensary	Rev. C. T. Perks
Richmond and East Melbourne Ladies' Benevolent Society	Mrs. Henty-Wilson
Salvation Army	Commissioner Coombes
Society for Assistance of Persons of Education	Mr. Lloyd Taylor
Society of St. Vincent de Paul	Mr. C. H. Grondona
South Yarra Home	Mr. J. W. Veal
St. Kilda Ladies' Benevolent Society	Miss Jennings
Swiss Society of Victoria	Marcus von Steiger
Victorian Deaf and Dumb Institution	Rev. Dr. Watkin
Victorian Eye and Ear Hospital	Mr. E. M. Gibbs
Victorian Infant Asylum	Mrs. Arthur Nicholls
Victoria Stiftung	*Rev. H. Herlitz*
Women's Hospital	Mrs. Munce
Young Men's Christian Association	Rev. J. M. Edwards
Young Women's Christian Association	Mrs. Skinner

(Charity Organisation Society, *Annual Report*, Melbourne, 1896, inside cover)

• This is a list of all the charitable agencies operating in late nineteenth-century Melbourne. What does it suggest about the needs of the city's poor?

Prostitution

The case of the widow and her disreputable-looking man, mentioned previously, was possibly a reference to prostitution. This was one of the few 'professions' open to women when other opportunities for employment were denied them. The story of 'Annie Jenkin' is typical of many. For much of the 1930s, she tried to make a living as a bookkeeper and barmaid. She claimed that neither occupation paid her enough to keep herself 'decently'.

It was the social system of Australia that forced me to work for myself [she recalled]. [Only] when I could not get a decent living wage anywhere else, [did I go] to work in a Roe Street brothel.

For Annie, this decision meant working full-time in a brothel tolerated by the police near the centre of Perth. It involved handing over half her earnings to the 'madam' who managed the brothel and undergoing regular medical inspections for venereal disease. And there could be no easy going back—working on Roe Street meant wide public notoriety, and regular employers were reluctant to give women jobs when they knew they had been prostitutes.
(See Documents 4.5, 4.6 and 4.7.)

The decision to become a prostitute had not always involved such an 'all-or-nothing' commitment. In the nineteenth century, it was much easier for women to work part-time as prostitutes, supplementing meagre wages by occasionally taking a man to a

'The snares of city life'. World War I (1914–1918) was a period of heightened concern about the moral threats to Australia's womanhood.

(Central Methodist Mission, *Report*, 1915, in Ann O'Brien, *Poverty's Prison: the Poor in New South Wales 1880-1918*, Melbourne University Press, 1988, p. 122)

DOCUMENT 4.5

Children in brothels

(Report Sergeant Egglestone, 10 August 1900, Perth Police Files)

• What is Sergeant Egglestone's attitude to children living with their mothers in brothels? Do you think the mothers would share his opinion?

(Evidence of Mrs Agnes Milne, shirtmaker, Shops and Factories Royal Commission, South Australia, 1892)

Julia M—, a prostitute who habituates the Chinese quarters and resides in a lane off Murray Street known as the Cowyard, has a son eight years of age residing with her. Mrs G— who keeps a house of ill-fame in the same locality has two daughters aged respectively ten and sixteen years both of whom reside with her. Both these houses are frequented by Chinese, Malays and Afghans and the scenes nightly witnessed in the locality amongst such associations render homes such as described most undesirable for children.

Mrs S— keeps a house of ill-repute in Murray Street she has a son thirteen years of age living with her. Nelly B— an half caste Aboriginal also residing in Murray Street under similar circumstances has a male child seven months old.

Mary R—, Murray St, has a son 5 years old . . . they all look healthy.

DOCUMENT 4.6

An honest living?

4375. How many houses of ill-fame do you know of in which shirts are taken in? — I only know of one. Others we cannot prove.

4376. Was the proof satisfactory to you? — Yes.

4377. Do you think there are many more? — Well, I have been told so by several, but I have not had it proved to me.

4378. Do you think there are a dozen such places? — On the good authority of a gentleman, I believe there are dozens. He said it was a common thing to see "dress-making done here," and "shirt-making wanted" in the windows.

4379. Do you think the work done is sufficient to materially affect the prices paid for shirt-making in Adelaide? — It does affect them. This is one thing that helps to keep the prices down.

4380. Do you think that in these houses they make one shirt a day for every other 100 made in Adelaide? — I do not know about the proportion.

4381. Have you any reason to believe they make more than 1 per cent? — No; I do not believe they do.

4382. Then that would not affect the price very much? — Yes; it affects it in this way: The ware-houses say, "We can get it done at such a price, and you must do it at that."

4383. Can they not get it done at such a price in this place? — No; they cannot. A great deal of the work is spoilt, and dozens of the shirts have to be undone and other women have to be paid for doing them again.

4384. Do you suggest that Parliament should take steps to prevent women from making shirts and earning money in this way? — Yes; I should think so.

4385. The making of a shirt in itself is making money in an honest way, and you suggest that these women earn money in a less desirable way? — Yes.

4386. If you take away the honest way you will encourage them in the other way? — They only have this work as a blind.

4387. How would you decide this question? — By a board.

4388. Do not you think it would take a long time to decide whether a woman living in a house of ill-fame should be allowed to make shirts? — It might, but a board should decide it. This moral question is one of the greatest questions of the day. If it could be proved that the house was not an honest place the licence should be refused.

4389. If the board said they were not to get honest work what would you do? — If they leave that house they can get honest work.

4390. Do you think that before any woman should be allowed to earn her living at sewing she should be subjected to examination as to her moral character? — Yes; I would.

4391. Would it not be extremely heart-breaking to an ordinary honest woman to have to go through an investigation of that sort to prove that she was virtuous before a Parliamentary board? — You cannot connect the honest woman with the woman who keeps a house of ill-fame.

DOCUMENT 4.6 CONTINUED

6854.   Do you think it would be an interference if, after you have said a woman is proper to do work, the Government inspector said she should not do it? — That would depend on the basis the inspector was acting upon.

6855.   Do you think it would be right on any basis? — I should think it would be possibly right. One could not express an opinion, not knowing what rules and regulations the inspector had behind him.

6856.   The basis I refer to would be as to a woman's moral character? — I do not see what it has to do with her capacity or incapacity for making shirts. I do not see that a woman whose character is not good could not be allowed to make shirts. It might help to keep her from immorality. You might make those who are bad worse if you said you shall not try to make an honest living.

(Evidence Mr G. A. Hodges, Manager, D. & W. Murray's Shirt and Hat Department, Shops and Factories Royal Commission, South Australia, 1892)

• Why do Mrs Milne and Mr Hodges disagree as to whether prostitutes should be allowed to make shirts?

Salvation Army Rescue Home, Brisbane. Christian philanthropists attempted to 'save' so-called 'fallen' women by providing them with moral and practical retraining. Would the skills imparted in this home provide women with an economic alternative to prostitution?

(*Boomerang*, 9 February 1889)

DOCUMENT 4.7

Prostitutes, the police and the public

It is time those people of ill-fame was not fined again there's one girl from Roe Street Regular makes a practise of coming up to Fitzgerald Street only in her bloomers and singlet . . . and only as a coat for a sham comes up where people children are kicking the football the coat flys open nothing only pants singlet on its time they were stopped a common occurrence where the children to see her . . . and those others singing out to every man passes.

they want fining Heavy

Low things

Disgusted

• • • •

I have to report that the Brothels in Roe St have received a considerable amount of attention during the past three months, during that period six convictions have been obtained . . .

I might state that the conditions in Roe St for some time have been very hard, there is not one house that can meet their expenses and the girls generally are having a very lean time, this to a certain extent has had a tendency to bring some of them to the gates to try and get the necessary money to carry on with. These houses are receiving constant attention from the Plain Clothes Police.

• • • •

Might I suggest that you use every ounce of your power to shift the brothels along the railway frontage from West Perth to Perth? For years this has been an outstanding disgrace to our State and is undoubtedly most disquieting that such should exist, alongside the State's front door.

• • • •

When many of us bought property several years ago there was no question of the respectability of James and Charles Sts. Unscrupulous owners have let property for three times its value for this purpose, and the rest of us are unable to let our property . . .

• • • •

As an Officer of the Police Department for the past 35 years . . . I do consider that brothels are a necessary evil in so much as I think they are the greater buffer and safeguard against minimal offences against females and girls of slender years . . .

Regarding the children from St. Brigid's school—the inmates of Roe Street complain about children throwing missiles and using insulting words to the girls. These children do not need to pass along Roe St to get to the station.

. . . one of the main things adopted at these houses is cleanliness and if a girl shows any sign of disorder she is sent straight away to the Doctor and is not allowed to resume business till thoroughly well, not so the numerous well dressed harlots around they can carry on with impunity, and it is almost impossible to convict them of any offence.

(Letter to Perth Police from local resident, 26 June 1931)

(Report P. C. C. [Plain Clothes Constable] Culmsee to C. I. O'Halloran, 23 June 1932)

(Letter forwarded by Secretary for Railways to Police Commissioner, 9 July 1932)

(Deputation of property owners to Minister of Police, 30 July 1933)

(Report P. C. C. Culmsee, 16 August 1934)

• All of the above extracts were taken from the Perth Police File on the Roe Street brothels in the 1930s. What do they say about the pressures on prostitutes in these brothels during these years? In what ways were the problems they experienced similar to those of women in 'straight' occupations? In what ways were they different? Do you think people's attitudes to prostitution have changed since the 1930s?

park at night. Or women could move in and out of prostitution, working for a few weeks or months when they could not get work at their regular occupations.

(See Documents 4.8 and 4.9.)

Between 1870 and 1930 new laws and police practices to deal with prostitution made it increasingly difficult for women to 'rise' once they had 'fallen'. Police kept lists of brothels and prostitutes and in some states insisted they have regular medical checks for venereal disease. Once on these lists, it was hard for women to convince the police that their names should be removed. The growth of organised crime also made it harder for women to leave a life of prostitution or to do it on a casual basis. This was especially so when criminal gangs were also involved with illegal drugs, as was the case with Kate Leigh's notorious gang in Sydney in the 1920s and 1930s. She was known as 'The Snow Queen' because of her involvement in the cocaine trade. Girls and women brought to Australia as prostitutes from poor parts of Japan, Italy and France in the late nineteenth and early twentieth centuries were especially vulnerable; they were often without friends and unable to speak enough English to allow them to leave their supervised lives in the brothels. At the same time, Australian society became less tolerant of street soliciting, so that women who had previously worked as freelancers on the streets were forced to work in brothels for 'madams', where they had much less freedom and often earned less. These changes benefited some women, especially the successful madams, but for others they were disastrous. The life histories of Tilly Devine and 'Lily Earnshaw' illustrate these contrasting fates.

DOCUMENT 4.8

A new development

Amongst the many strange things that occurred in 'The Boom' period—1888 to 1891—there was nothing stranger than the appearance of a number of young women—hawkers of trinkets and such-like wares—going about from one place of business to another. They were got up in the attire of nurses, and were exceedingly pertinacious and forward. Complaints even of improprieties of a serious kind reached me, but there was a difficulty in getting evidence. Inspector Joe Brown was at this time doing uniform duty in the city, and all licensing business was in his charge. I desired him to announce that all hawkers should provide themselves with the necessary licence from the Court of Petty Sessions. There was immediately a long list of applicants. Brown was instructed to oppose them all on the ground that it was reported that the applicants were not genuine traders, and that in any case the police required time to make inquiries as to character, etc. I remember that Brown did not quite like the job, but he carried out his part so well that there was a sudden stampede from the court of all applicants, and the trouble came to an end.

(J. Sadlier, *Recollections of a Victorian Police Officer*, George Robertson, Melbourne, 1913, p. 250)

• What does this policeman believe these women were really selling? Why do you think they dressed as nurses?

DOCUMENT 4.9

A dangerous life

I beg to report for your information that Marguerite Du Four—a French girl—who led a dissolute life in this state for several years was fatally shot in a brothel known as 'San Joy' on the 3rd December, 1910, and that she died in the Perth Public Hospital on the following day . . . the man who shot her was tried for murder . . . found guilty of manslaughter and sentenced to 12 months hard labour.

• • • •

'Cecilia R— came to her death in a cell at the Fremantle Police Lockup on the morning of the 26th March, 1913 from heart failure Supervening on Pleurisy and Pneumonia, in accordance with the medical testimony. No blame is attachable to anyone.

• • • •

'The only death in the Fremantle area from Venereal Disease in the last three years was that of Margaret M—, an habitual prostitute, who died in the Fremantle Hospital . . .

• • • •

I have to report that at about 9.15 pm, I was on duty in Market Street when Councillor Wakely reported to me that the soldiers were at 'Mary Anns' a brothel in Bannister Street smashing up the place with pickets . . . We proceeded to Mary Ann Collins in Bannister St and found about 6 soldiers there, three of them mad drunk, with pickets which they had pulled off the fence and were trying to smash in through the wire lattice . . .

(Letter, Detective Sergeant L. Condon to Inspector of Police, Perth, 7 April 1911, the information to be passed on to her mother in France who had not heard from her daughter for six months)

(Inquest Report on Cecilia R—, age 42, prostitute)

(Report of Registrar of Deaths to Fremantle Municipal Council, November 1913)

(Report of Sergeant H. Jones, Fremantle, 7 April 1918)

• The above reports from the Perth Police Files tell of some of the hazards encountered by prostitutes in the course of their work. Do you think other women workers faced such threats?

Tilly Devine: 'Queen of the Underworld'

Matilda Mary Devine (Tilly) arrived in Sydney in 1919 at the age of eighteen, having married an Australian soldier in England. Together they started work in the Liverpool Street area of East Sydney. Tilly's husband, Jim, found the customers and she looked after them. She was regularly arrested by the police and paid up to fifteen pounds in fines each month, but continued to make a good living despite this. In 1921 she bought an expensive Cadillac which Jim drove while she solicited from the back seat.

By 1925 Tilly had had over eighty convictions and numerous fights with different underworld people. She first went to prison in that year for slashing a man with a razor. When she came out, she opened a brothel in Palmer Street and during the next few years she and Jim were both heavily involved in gangland fighting. The police, however, had ceased to bother her, despite plenty of evidence that she was involved in this fighting as well as extortion, gambling, drugs and the supply of illegal liquor. She was probably bribing them to leave her alone, and frightening witnesses so that even had she been charged more frequently it is unlikely she would have been convicted. By the end of the 1930s she was a wealthy woman, in a position to open up and run twenty brothels during World War II and so turn her wealth into a fortune.

'Lily Earnshaw': Disease, destitution and drugs

Lily's career as a prostitute started to turn bad when she was arrested in Kalgoorlie on a charge of vagrancy in 1914. She served four months in Fremantle gaol and on her release went to work in a brothel in Perth. In February the following year the Government Medical Officer, who was at this time unofficially examining brothel inmates every two weeks, reported to the police that she was suffering from venereal disease. The police constable sent to investigate reported:

On my arrival (at the brothel) 'Lily Earnshaw' was just leaving. She was drunk and I detained her until P. C. Donoghue came up. When he questioned her she stated that she had been doing business at the house and was suffering from 'clap'. She said that she had been turned out of the house mentioned and did not know where she would go to. We arrested her on a charge of drunkenness and further charged her with having no lawful visible means of support. On being searched she only had threepence in her possession.

On this occasion she was sentenced to six months' imprisonment, the usual legal response to diseased prostitutes. She spent ten months of the next two years in gaol, again officially for 'vagrancy' but in reality because she had venereal disease. By 1919 she was associating with 'disreputable' Chinese and was arrested occasionally for drunkenness and disorderly conduct. She was said to be an opium addict.

Baby-farming and abortion

Prostitution was not the only form of work thought to imperil a girl's morality. In the nineteenth century, in particular, baby-farming provided a necessary but socially undesirable service for many overburdened mothers. At its best, baby-farming was a form of extended child-care. (Creches were not established until the early twentieth century and even then were beyond the means of most working women.) For a few pounds or even shillings, a mother could hand her infant over to a woman willing to 'support' the child. This would leave the mother free to work in a factory or in service (neither industry tolerated the presence of children). Farming out one's young was also a form of economising. Unable to feed those she had, a desperate mother might well assign another hungry mouth to a baby-farmer. Technically, when circumstances improved, the family could be reunited.

But such reunions were uncommon. The life cycle of a working-class family meant that months or even years might pass before a mother could afford to reclaim her infant. By that time the child may have died, as infant mortality rates were alarmingly high in the nineteenth century and separation from a nursing and watchful mother narrowed already slender chances of survival. Many deaths were accidental; inexperienced baby-farmers fed their charges food which choked them, and dropped, knocked or smothered them. But others were not. A growing child ate into the baby-farmer's small commission; and early death saved both money and trouble. Moreover, murder through neglect was easily concealed from a coroner. Children died of colds caught when their bedclothes were taken from them, or wasted away for want of proper sustenance. The most notorious of the baby-farmers was Mrs Frances Knorr, executed on three separate charges of infanticide in 1894. According to the prosecution, Mrs Knorr had strangled the babies in her care, mutilated the bodies and buried their remains in her garden.

Victorian society was outraged at the whole baby-farming industry and these murders in particular. But blaming individuals distracted attention from the real causes of these social problems. So long as women had to work to support themselves and their dependants without access to affordable, suitable child-care, children would be vulnerable in the hands of unbalanced or unscrupulous people like Mrs Knorr. Hanging Mrs Knorr did nothing to solve the problem.

(See Document 4.10.)

A similar argument could be adopted in regard to abortion. Until recent years women have been denied control over their reproductive capacity. The sale of contraceptive devices was illegal for much of the nineteenth century, and as late as the 1930s safe and effective contraception was really only available to the wealthy. Consequently, families grew well beyond the means of their

DOCUMENT 4.10

Baby-farming

5 October 1890

Admitted: Wakefield, Annie   6 months

Dunne, Alameda   8 months

Malony, Alexander   3 months

No. 2 Police writes, 'They were found in the care of Susannah Bourke, 66, Glebe who has been taken into custody on suspicion of causing the death of a child.' The manager's report on baby farming received by the House Committee on Tuesday giving details of visit to Mrs Bourke's house wherein 9 infants were discovered . . .

Agnes Dunn, unmarried, calls and states that Alameda Dunn is her offspring and she gave it to Mrs Bourke for adoption for life for £5; That Mrs Bourke stated she was acting for a Mrs Ingram who would take the child to England as her own child and that eventually the child would be worth thousands Mr Ingram being fabulously wealthy. Agnes Dunn works for Doris and Co, Shirtmakers, Bond Street. The putative father of the child is George Collier, bricklayer, whereabouts unknown. The child is in the care of a married sister Sarah Ann Dunn, Avery Street, North Shore. The following is a copy of the receipt for adoption.

> September 22 1890
>
> Received from Mrs Dunn £1 stirling on account of a child's adoption
>
> Balance £4 to be paid by weekly instalments of 10 shillings.
>
> (Signed) Mrs Bourke
>
> pro Mrs Ingram
>
> 8 October 1890
>
> Dunn, Alameda
>
> Discharged to the mother and her Aunt Mrs Dunn; 3 Avery Street, North Shore
>
> The Rev Mr Yarmount sends a strong recommendation of Mrs Dunn's fitness to care for the child.

(Extracted from the *Inmates Journal* of the Benevolent Society of New South Wales, Mitchell Library, Sydney, ML 240)

• Why did Agnes Dunn place her child in Mrs Bourke's care?

parents. Abortion was the last resort for women who were desperate to avoid having more children. Today abortion is safe and relatively painless; in those days it was neither. By making the operation illegal, moralists and medical authorities drove the abortionists to backyards and drawing-rooms. There they could charge what they liked for their services and disregard the health of their patients. Fifty years later, Jean Brett recalled the fear and the pain:

The baby bonus *by Norman Lindsay. In 1912 the Australian Commonwealth Government began paying five pounds to mothers on the birth of each child to encourage population growth. This is a rare instance of women receiving monetary reward for the reproductive labour of child-bearing. As this cartoon shows, its payment to the mother was official recognition that male breadwinners did not always use their 'family' wage to support their dependants.*

(*Bulletin*, 22 August 1912. Copyright Jane Glad)

THE BABY BONUS.

MRS. SLINK (*flourishing £5 note*): "No, Clarence Henry, yer don't get a penny THIS time, if I know it! Yer boozed the twins, but yer ain't goin' to swaller Augustus!"

[It was] damned agony . . . you'd have no anaesthetic, no nothing, and all they would do is just clean your womb out and you would be conscious . . . I had no idea either, I don't know what I expected but you do think they are going to do something . . . something gentle, don't you? No, they don't. They just scrape it out as though [they were] scraping up mud out of a gutter. That's the truth. They had no feelings, no feelings whatever. You paid whatever sum it was, it was far more than a man's weekly wage would be. Some women couldn't have any more kids after that. As I say they scraped you out, like scraping out the inside of a marrow.

Not all women suffered such grim options and dreadful experiences. Beyond the poverty, beyond the margins, many women achieved respectability and even comfort, while a few rose to positions of power and responsibility. They are the concern of the next few chapters.

Notes

Nyungar girl—Unnamed girl, 'The stockrider's daughter', in Jan Carter, *Nothing to Spare: Recollections of Australian Pioneering Women*, Penguin, Ringwood, 1986, pp. 19–32.

Daisy Corunna—Sally Morgan, *My Place*, Fremantle Arts Centre Press, 1988, p. 334.

Clarinna Stringer—Bruce Scates, 'A struggle for survival: unemployment and the unemployed agitation in late nineteenth century Melbourne', *Australian Historical Studies*, Vol. 24, No. 94, April 1990, pp. 57–8.

Annie Jenkin—Evidence to Royal Commission into the Administration of the Perth City Council, 1938, pp. 844–5. Manuscript held at Parliament House, Perth.

Kate Leigh, Tilly Devine—Judith Allen, 'The making of a prostitute proletariat in New South Wales', in K. Daniels (ed.), *So Much Hard Work: Prostitution in Australian History*, Harper Collins, U.K., 1984, pp. 192–232.

'Lily Earnshaw'—Report of P. C. Pike, 8 July 1915, quoted by Sub-Inspector Mitchell in Evidence to the Royal Commission into Allegations Against Dr Blanchard, Chief Secretary's Office File 1083/1915, Battye Library, Perth.

Jean Brett—Rhonda Wilson, *The Good Talk*, Penguin, Ringwood, 1985, p. 20.

SUGGESTIONS FOR STUDY

For discussion

1 In today's cities, which people are most likely to be in poverty, 'on the margins' of the paid economy? Are these the same as the groups of people most vulnerable in the period 1860–1939?

2 What financial assistance is there for destitute and unemployed people today? Is it adequate?

3 We saw how in periods of depression, when a lot of people were unemployed, communities worked together to help each other survive. They exchanged various goods and services in an informal economy. Can people do similar sorts of things today?

4 What are the laws governing prostitution in this state now? How do you think the life of a prostitute today compares with this earlier period?

5 Being poor before 1939 could be described as a health hazard. Why? Has this changed?

To write about

1 Imagine you are an Aboriginal woman taken from your people to work for a white family in the city in 1920. How do you view your employers and how do they view you? Other domestics could escape service, either through marriage or by finding work elsewhere. Are the same options open to you?

2 The Ladies Benevolent Society was a charitable organisation. Before giving assistance, however, each case was assessed by an investigation to determine if it was really both needy and 'deserving'. Write two reports such an investigation might have produced during in the 1890s depression: the first dealing with a case considered deserving; the second with one which was considered undeserving.

3 You are the man or woman deemed 'undeserving' by the investigation in question 2.
a Write a letter to the Ladies Benevolent Society appealing against their decision not to help you.
b Given that you have been denied relief, how will you manage to survive?

4 What child-care facilities were/are available for your mother, and her mother before her? Are these facilities any cheaper or any more accessible for the average family today than they have been in the past?

5 In Victoria, papers presented to Parliament in the 1891 session tabled the following information, revealing that mothers in 'indigent circumstances' were the dominant parental group of children in reform schools in June 1891.

Children in reform schools 1891

	Fathers	Mothers	Total
Dead	95	104	199
Deserted	104	23	127
Unknown	45	21	66
In other colonies	15	3	18
In England	1	–	1
In indigent circumstances	124	238	362
In fair circumstances	22	7	29
In hospital	–	7	7
In lunatic asylums	7	8	15
In gaol	26	21	47
Mothers prostitutes	–	7	7
Total	439	439	878

a Graph these data.

b What percentage of the parents were 'women in indigent circumstances'?

c Which is the highest male category? How would you account for such a high male percentage?

d What assumptions are built into the label 'in indigent circumstances' by the compiler of the table or you the reader? Are they valid?

e What does indigent mean? Look it up in a dictionary.

Community resources

Community services

1 Volunteer to help a charitable agency for the poor in the evening or over a weekend. What sort of people do they deal with and what circumstances have compelled them to look for aid? Does the agency still distinguish between deserving and undeserving cases? Do the poor themselves have any chance of permanently improving their lot?

2 Invite a representative of the Aboriginal and Torres Strait Islander Commission or other Aboriginal group to speak to your class. What particular problems do Aboriginal women face in achieving economic independence? How has their situation, particularly employment prospects, changed over the past two hundred years?

3 Visit the local office of your Department of Social Security. Find out what pensions and services are available for:
   • Aboriginal women on a low income;
   • deserted wives with children;
   • unemployed women in the three age groups: under 18, 18–40, 40–60;
   • aged and invalid women;
   • women on low incomes with large dependent families.

Imagine you fall into one of these categories. Bearing in mind the size of your pension, draw up a weekly budget for yourself (and your family). Can you manage financially? How could you supplement your income? How do the support services offered today differ from those which functioned in the past?

4 Draw up a survival chart for women on the margins of society. Include the location of women's refuges, rape crisis centres, charitable agencies and cheap places to eat and sleep. Compare your chart with the index to charities reproduced in Document 4.4 'Charity Directory'. Which groups and situations are catered for now which were overlooked in the past? Are the facilities adequate in either case?

5 Commerce and Public Administration

Shop work

The drapery stores which supplied Eleanor with cloth to make into garments offered other employment opportunities to women: they employed women to sell their products as well as to make them. And as the nineteenth century progressed, the number of these jobs increased. Drapery stores gradually diversified into the sale of other sorts of goods—hardware, groceries and sporting goods, for instance—until they became huge 'emporiums', or department stores. The well-known firms of Grace Brothers and David Jones began in this way in the late nineteenth century.

Although at the beginning drapery shops relied almost entirely on the assistance of members of the proprietor's family, as they grew larger this was clearly impossible: they had to employ outsiders as well. But even firms employing hundreds or even thousands of workers tried very hard to keep up their image as 'family firms' and the stern figure of the floorwalker not only ensured that customers were suitably attended to but also kept a fatherly eye on the shop assistants. This was important, since shop proprietors relied on the more respectable image of their workplace to attract girls who might otherwise go into factory work. The image of the family business, rather than that of capitalist enterprise, was also important in keeping good relations with the buying public; many customers were more inclined to shop with stores which had a reputation for treating their employees well than with those which obviously exploited their workers.

But while shop work might have been respectable, it was not the easy work some might have imagined. Nineteenth-century shops opened for very long hours (up to nine and ten at night was usual, six days of the week) and assistants had to remain standing for the entire working day. Nor were rates of pay always better than factory work, while shop assistants had to keep up a much higher standard of dress and personal appearance. None of these things seemed to deter workers from seeking work in shops: the number of shop assistants in Australia increased sevenfold

*T'othersiders Shop, Eastern
Goldfields (WA), circa 1890.
Women played an important part in
the economic and social life of the
goldfields in all parts of Australia.
The women shown here were among
the many who ran small shops.*

(Battye Library, 1485B)

*Mrs Greenwood's Temperance
Dining Rooms, Mertondale, WA,
1902. In the mainly masculine
world of gold rush towns, some
women made a business of
providing services which in other
situations men's wives and mothers
performed 'for love'.*

(Eastern Goldfields Historical Society,
49/1A)

between 1891 and 1921, with most of the new recruits being
women and girls. By 1911 there were more females than males
employed in Australia's shops. Indeed, parents were so keen to
get their children into these jobs that they offered their services
free or even paid employers to take them on and teach them a
'trade'. The employers were only too willing to oblige, especially
in employing females, since they could be paid less than half the
male rate for doing basically the same work. A few recruits did in
fact learn the trade and advance from humble assistant to
department head or buyer, but the vast majority never left the
counters. This was especially true for women, who could advance
only within a very limited range of 'female' departments such as
ladies' clothing and drapery. As big stores became even bigger in
the twentieth century, the promotional opportunities for women
compared to men decreased further; men could move into the
executive levels of the company while most women remained
confined to sales work. Meanwhile, in the suburbs and in country
towns, thousands of women continued working in small and
medium-sized shops, their work little different to that performed
in similar places fifty years earlier.

(See Documents 5.1 and 5.2.)

The twentieth century did bring some changes to shop work.
As a result of government intervention, shopping hours were
universally reduced and conditions improved. Shop proprietors
were now required to provide seats for their workers, even if the
assistants were still too frightened to use them lest the
floorwalker glance in their direction! In the 1920s and 1930s many
of the big stores also became involved in 'welfare' schemes for
their employees. They provided dining-rooms, social activities,
sporting clubs, free medical attention and free educational classes.
While these services may have been aimed at avoiding hostile

DOCUMENT 5.1

Standing in the shop

Miss -------,

18 Mar., 1891

2512.   *By the Chairman :* What is your occupation? I am an assistant behind the counter.
2513.   In a draper's establishment? Yes.
2514.   How long have you been at that employment? A year and five months.
2515.   All the time at the same place? Yes.
2516.   Did you begin there as an apprentice? No; I had been a little time at it before.
2517.   Elsewhere? Yes.
2518.   What wages did you get when you commenced? I got 5s. when I first started.
2519.   What are you getting now? 9s.
2520.   How old are you? Twenty.
2521.   Do you live with your parents or board out? I am living with a married sister.
2522.   Do you pay her for your board? No; I should not be able to.
2523.   I suppose your agreement is a verbal one with your employer? Yes.
2524.   How long have you been getting 9s.? About three months.
2525.   At what time do you begin work? At a quarter to 9.
2526.   And leave off when? I work three nights a week; two nights up till 9 p.m., and on Saturday until 10 p.m. and after. Very often I have to work until 10.20 p.m., and often later.
2527.   How far have you to travel when you leave your work? To Woolloongabba.
2528.   Are any holidays allowed to you? Not unless we take them ourselves. We are not paid for them.
2529.   Are any holidays allowed to you during the year? No.
2530.   If you are away through sickness do you get paid for the time? No; if it is only for one day it is not deducted; but if it is for longer the wages are deducted.
2531.   When you were getting 5s. were you taught your business and shown what to do? I had to pick it up myself.
2532.   Then really you were doing the work of another person at 5s. a week? Yes.
2533.   Is there a room for you to have meals in? Yes.

2656.   Are you satisfied with your present wages? No.
2657.   You think you are worth more? Yes.
2658.   *By the Chairman:* Have you applied to Mr. Williams for higher wages? The last rise I got I should have got more, but he told me times were bad.
2659.   *By Mr. Chapman :* Have you found Mr. Williams to be tyrannical with you or other employees— bullying, cross, or scolding? On some occasions.
2660.   With you? Yes.
2661.   For neglect of duty? On one or two occasions.
2662.   You are very comfortable in Mr. Williams's employ? I like the place well enough, but the wages are very small, and I do not like working at night.
2663.   *By Dr. Booth :* Have you ever suffered from the effects of overwork? I have felt it on several occasions.
2664.   In what way have you felt it? The gas is very trying.
2665.   Has it given you a headache? Yes.
2666.   Has it interfered with you in any other way — with your digestion? No.
2667.   Don't you think that walking to and fro between home and the shop would improve your health? I would rather ride after standing all day.
2668.   *By Mr. Dalrymple :* You say you do not get your wages paid at specified periods? No.
2669.   Do you get them paid when you ask, and are you expected to ask before being paid? I have never asked.
2670.   You say the gas injuriously affected your health. Would it have affected your health if you had been at home, or is it merely the gas in the shop that is injurious? The shop is very close.

(Evidence of an unnamed female shop assistant, Shops, Factories and Workshops Royal Commission, Brisbane, *Queensland Parliamentary Papers*, 1891, Vol. II)

• Why does this female shop assistant ask for her name to be withheld? What does her testimony tell us about a shop assistant's working life?

DOCUMENT 5.2

A Brisbane doctor's views on shop work

12667. *By Mrs. Cooper:* Do you think that long standing for many years would cause more serious ailments in a woman's frame than in a man's? Decidedly a man can stand it much better.

12668. But do you not think it might cause not only present but future suffering in a woman? It might unfit her altogether for married life.

12669. The consequences might be permanent injury? Yes; possibly.

12670. Would long hours of confinement and working under gaslight have a more injurious effect on a woman's constitution than a man's? I don't think it would. I think women can stand confinement and bad air quite as well as men.

12671. Do you think that the production of healthy young citizens is the most important thing for the State to consider? I think it is very important as well to find work for them when they are produced.

12672. But is it not an important thing that healthy children should be produced? It is very important, but I would not say it is the only important thing.

12673. But the State cannot continue if the supply of citizens does not exist? Citizens cannot exist if the work is not here for them to exist by.

12674. Will weakly women be likely to produce healthy children? No; that is very unlikely.

12675. Would you consider that anything which is likely to injure the health of a large class of women is a matter of public concern? Certainly, it concerns the State.

12676. Would you think the evils of long hours and continuous standing are sufficiently important to warrant State interference on the ground that the health of the women being interfered with the children who are born cannot be healthy? I think it is necessary for the State to interfere in a matter of that kind, because although some employers are very considerate and careful of their employees, others are the reverse.

12704. Have you had any experience in the southern colonies? Yes. I was resident surgeon in the Melbourne Hospital.

12705. Do you think the climate of Queensland is more trying to persons who have to work indoors than the climate of Victoria or New South Wales? I think so. The heat is more trying.

12706. Then the hours worked here should be less than in Victoria? Yes; the strain would be greater on people here for the same number of hours than in Victoria.

12743. Will you tell the Commission what diseases women and young girls are liable to in consequence of so much standing? I will if the Commission wish me to. What makes me regard the practice of standing as so injurious to women is that it causes displacement of the womb, and in this climate that complaint is exceedingly prevalent, and is aggravated by the heat. The general tone of the muscular tissue is relaxed by the continued heat, and the standing is the more unfortunate thing that a young girl can be subject to. I think it is a cruel thing to ask a young girl to stand all the time while at work in the shop. In fact, I do not know of any greater cruelty that is allowed. Then, again, of course, hemorrhoids, or piles, and constipation are brought about, and pretty equally affect both sexes. I think employers should be forced to provide seats for young girls, for the reason I mention. I do not think we can treat the matter too seriously when we know the amount of suffering that is caused.

12744. I observe both in New South Wales and Victoria medical testimony condemns very strongly the practice of making young girls stand while at work? I have not read anything on the subject, but I am quite satisfied from my own experience that the practice is injurious, and in this hot climate the danger is very much increased.

12745. Then you think the practice unfits women very considerably for married life? Decidedly. It tends to unfit them for married or any other kind of life.

12746. And it would undoubtedly be an ultimate injury to the race? I think so, certainly.

12747. With regard to the closets for males and females, do you think they should be distinctly apart, and that different passages should lead to each? Certainly, out of sight of each other, and the entrances out of sight. There can be no second opinion on the subject. Plenty of females will simply not pay attention to natural calls on account of the approaches to these places being overlooked.

12748. Have you known cases in which females have suffered from disease directly in consequence of their delicacy over these matters? Oh yes, there is no doubt about that. In many cases constipation and hemorrhoids have been caused by such neglect.

(Evidence of Dr J. H. Little, Shops, Factories and Workshops Royal Commission, Brisbane, *Queensland Parliamentary Papers*, 1891, Vol. II)

• What does Dr Little consider to be the main health hazards associated with shop work? What remedy does he suggest? Does he share the concern of Royal Commissioner, Mrs Cooper, about women's health? What does his evidence suggest about the different experiences of shop work from one part of Australia to another?

union activity and customer boycotts, they also meant that these shops became much more pleasant places in which to work. This approach to staff relations was certainly very different to the more authoritarian system reported in a Melbourne store before World War I.

(See Document 5.3.)

DOCUMENT 5.3

Ball and Welch's fine list

The following is a list of the fines imposed upon employees of that firm:

Substituting goods ordered without advising, 1s.

Omitting to notify office as required, 2s 6d.

For being late in the morning, for each five minutes or fraction of five minutes after the first five minutes allowed as grace, 6d.

For each five minutes or fraction of five minutes, without any allowance for grace, 6d.

Leaving by any other door except the east door, 10s.

Not having the amount tendered on top of bill, 6d.

Omitting mode of delivery, 6d.

Incorrect, insufficient, or indistinct address on bills, 6d.

Omitting to get packer's initial, 6d.

Not having goods called back and bills signed, 6d.

Putting another assistant's number on bill as examined, 2s. 6d.

Approbation without folio and signature, 6d.

Approbation bills omitting folio and date, 6d.

Approbation slips without shopwalkers' signature, 6d.

Putting wrong department letter or omitting, 3d.

Omitting to pass credit for goods returned, whether entered or paid for, 10s.

For omitting to call assistance, 5s.

For omitting to enter in book, 1s.

For duplicates lost or missing, each, 1s.

Omitting to hand in checkbook, 6d.

Omitting to add index, 6d.

Incorrect addition of index, 3d.

Entering checks incorrectly, 3d.

Indistinct duplicates, 6d.

Incorrect, insufficient, or indistinct address slips, 6d.

Writing memos. or letters to customers privately, 1s.

Promising goods out of the ordinary delivery without the consent of the shopwalker, 1s.

Omitting to endorse orders with the required particulars, 6d.

Omitting to return letter orders to the office, 6d.

Omitting names of persons taking goods, 6d.

Cutting garments without counting-house signature, 1s.

For evading rule relating to employees' purchases, 1s.

For evading another rule relating to employees' purchases, 2s. 6d.

Laying aside goods, 2s. 6d.

Leaving goods improperly covered, 1s.

Omitting to return goods to their proper departments, 1s.

Using wax matches, 1s.

For omitting to bring articles left in shop to counting-house or secretary, 1s.

DOCUMENT 5.3 CONTINUED

Ball and Welch's Rule Book

Besides these fines, there are also 84 rules in the printed 'Rules and Regulations', issued to employees, and the breach of any one appears to be not only subject to fine but to dismissal. One rule, in fact, expressly states:

'Fines are imposed only for the purpose of maintaining commercial discipline, and must not be considered by assistants in the light of exoneration for the offence committed, and any assistant whose fine list is large, may expect to be asked to resign his or her position at any time.'

(*Tocsin*, 23 August 1900, p. 5)

• Why do you think this firm had such strict regulations and fines? If employers were to act unscrupulously, how could they use such a fine system to evade a legal minimum wage?

Shop assistants were not noted for their militancy or willingness to undertake collective action. Strikes were virtually unheard of and few workers took an interest in union affairs. Employees who felt their employers were not treating them fairly tended to take more individual kinds of action. Some bargained with employers to improve their own rates of pay, while many stole goods from the stores where they worked as a way of making up for their low wages. This was such a problem in the 1920s and 1930s that some department stores employed special detectives to spy on the employees.

By this time, however, department stores had other worries as well. Chain stores, such as G. J. Coles Pty Ltd, had appeared on the scene and quickly spread their branches throughout Australian cities, towns and suburbs. They sold a more limited range of products than the department stores and placed more importance on cheap prices than on quality or service. By the late 1930s, this style of selling was driving more conservative shops out of business. While the chain stores often meant financial ruin for their competitors, for shop assistants the consequences were also very serious. Their work became deskilled, in that they were required simply to exchange goods for money rather than utilise a wide knowledge of products in advising customers. Junior sales staff were just as effective as the more highly trained and were much cheaper, so there was much less opportunity for workers to advance within the store hierarchy. Workers often found that once they qualified for an adult wage they were sacked and cheaper junior staff taken on in their places.

Both department and chain stores took business away from small shops. Since many small shops were run by widows or married women, this trend also represented a decrease in opportunities for such women: the twentieth-century shop assistant was usually a young, single woman. Even when the big stores did employ married women, the conditions were such that mothers of young children could not easily have taken the work. In her own little shop, a mother could look after her children and

do a bit of housework while she waited for the door-bell to signal the arrival of customers in the adjoining shop. This made shopkeeping a popular occupation in the nineteenth century for women who had enough money to set up a small business of their own. But while the small shopkeeper found business declining in the late nineteenth and early twentieth centuries, new opportunities arose for women in office work.

Cash and Carry—ABC Store, Toogoolawah, Queensland, circa 1929. By the 1920s, women were firmly entrenched behind the counters in Australia's shops. What is the man in this photograph doing?

(Collection, John Oxley Library, Brisbane)

Postal and telegraph work

At first, it was the colonial governments that offered most scope for female employment. Mary Mahony, the widow of the main character in Henry Handel Richardson's novel, *The Fortunes of Richard Mahony*, declared that, 'There seems literally nothing a woman can do except teach and I'm too old for that. Nor have I the brains.' Instead, Mrs Mahony, like Richardson's own mother, secured a job as postmistress through her acquaintance with the Postmaster General. From 1870 to the end of the century, over half the post offices in Victoria were run by women. These were usually the widows or daughters of public servants who needed a respectable occupation to support themselves. A post office suited them very well, as it came with living quarters attached, so that the postmistress could move easily between her public and private roles and could maintain the more respectable image of someone who worked at home rather than one who 'went out' to work. From the government's point of view, employing these women as postmistresses was economical both because they could

Melbourne women telephonists, 1881. In the nineteenth century, the all-female environment of the telephone exchange provided light, clean, respectable work for young women of the middle class.

(*Australasian Sketches*, Telecom Australia)

be paid half the male salary and because by placing widows on the staff they did not have to worry about paying them a pension. Someone like Eleanor Hargreaves, of course, could not have taken on such a post: not only did she not have enough education, but she also had none of the connections with senior government officials which this system of appointment by patronage required.

In any case, such opportunities for women in postal and telegraph work dwindled at the turn of the twentieth century. Married women were the first to go, several colonial governments refusing to employ them after 1890. Victorian postmistresses and their female assistants organised in the 1890s to secure equal pay for the sexes—a concession granted to the few New South Wales postmistresses in 1895. Their campaign succeeded, but without the attraction of cheaper salaries, governments rarely employed women in these jobs again until the 1940s. Instead, they were confined to the new 'women's work' of attending telephone switchboards, the better paid and more promising opportunities within postal and telegraph work being reserved for men. Meanwhile, private enterprise opened its doors to female office workers.

Office work

Until the 1870s, colonial offices were staffed by men in suits who sat at tall stools, inkwell and quill at the ready. This type of colonial clerk was, however, much more than a transcriber of letters; he often composed the letters as well as writing them out neatly in impeccable copperplate, kept the firm's accounts, and made all sorts of decisions about the firm's business. Although not quite a modern-day executive, he was certainly a very different employee to the female clerk-typist who made her way into offices across Australia in the years between 1885 and 1920. At first typewriters were operated by both males and females, but it soon became obvious to employers that great savings could be made by having male clerks concentrate on certain types of work and leaving the typing to cheaper female office workers. The natural association between shorthand and typing meant that typists gradually took over this function as well. On 12 September 1911 the Melbourne *Age* commented on this move of women into office work:

Ten years ago it was the exception to find a woman employed as a clerk in any business establishment. Now it is the rule. Female clerks swarm in every town and city.

(See Document 5.4.)

Myer Emporium's Tube Room, 1920s. Department stores experimented with new methods of handling cash transactions in order to cope with the growing volume of sales. The tube system enabled sales assistants to send docket and cash to a separate room where clerks calculated and returned the change.

(The Myer Emporium Ltd Collection, The University of Melbourne Archives)

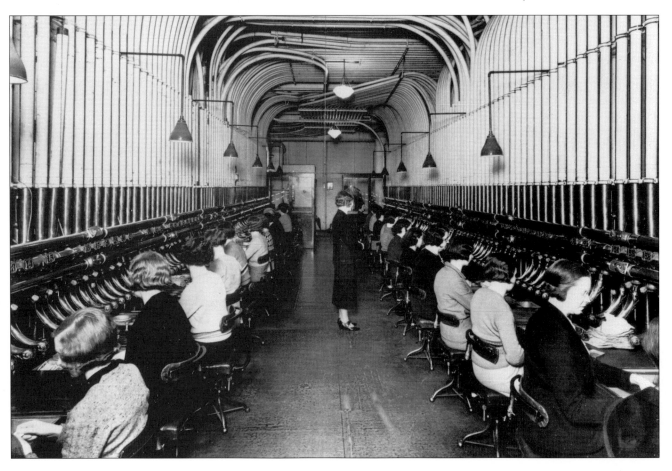

(*Western Australian Blue Books*, 1901–1914)

(Staff registers of the West Australian Bank [now Westpac] and the A.M.P. [new employees only are recorded] in G. Reekie, 'Female office workers in Western Australia, 1895–1920: the process of feminization and patterns of consciousness', in L. Layman (ed.) The *Workplace: Time Remembered Special Issue*, No. 5, 1982, Murdoch University.

DOCUMENT 5.4

Female office workers: some figures

Numbers of female and male typists/stenographers employed by the Western Australian Government 1901–1914

Year	Females	Males
1901	8	38
1905	7	14
1909	14	25
1914	74	24

Female clerks/typists/stenographers employed by the West Australian Bank and the Australian Mutual Provident Society (AMP) 1905–1919

Year	West Australian Bank	AMP
1905	–	2
1906	–	–
1907	–	1
1908	–	–
1909	–	1
1910	–	1
1911	–	5
1912	–	2
1913	–	5
1914	–	3
1915	5	5
1916	17	11
1917	20	13
1918	24	1
1919	26	2

• The above statistics show the different ways in which female workers were used in the public service and in the banks. What patterns emerge from these figures?

Once the 'feminisation' process had begun, it was self-sustaining: shorthand and typing became associated in people's minds with women's work, and therefore of lower status than male clerical work. Men entering commerce began to favour training in accountancy, law, commerce and advertising rather than typing and bookkeeping, thus leaving large areas of the field open to women at the lower levels.

Document 5.5 shows clearly how women's entry into offices had transformed men's work: women had not directly replaced men, but rather had come in as lower-status assistants who deferred to the authority of men.

Where did all these 'office girls' come from? Initially they came from families sufficiently well-off to pay for typing and/or shorthand courses at business colleges, but not so well-off that they could afford to keep their daughters at home in idleness. In some cases they were joined by wealthier girls who simply

DOCUMENT 5.5

The feminisation of office work

(*Sunday Times*, Perth, 7 February 1915, p. 6)

● What does this advertisement suggest about the changes that were taking place in Australian offices in the early twentieth century?

wanted to be independent or didn't like staying at home. The first female office workers were probably the daughters of prosperous skilled tradesmen or members of the lower middle-class—shopkeepers, teachers, clerks and so on. As time passed, the occupation attracted girls from more diverse backgrounds. The 1890s depression made even wealthy families realise the importance of having daughters with marketable skills, while the expansion of government-funded technical education in the decades which followed meant that girls from poorer backgrounds could also train in commercial subjects. By 1910 the practice of girls pursuing office work was quite well accepted by society. A woman who attended a small private boarding school at this time recalls the way in which stenography was regarded as almost the only prospect for girls of that class who needed to earn a living. Her experience also reflects the status of such female workers inside the office:

> At school, the pupils were very snobbish. The great idea was to get to England and be presented at Court . . . People took courses in shorthand and typing to fit them for jobs. I went to the technical college in Perth, for stenography, and obtained a job in an office, before I turned fifteen. I had a job in the office of an English mining engineer, whose Board of Directors was in England. I didn't use the typewriter well. I was always being called to book by the accountant; I wasn't allowed to take things straight into the boss which annoyed me . . . Women didn't have many opportunities, there weren't many jobs available.

Gibsonia Woollen Mills, Engineers' Workshop Office, 1922. By the 1920s, manufacturing firms employed working-class women in their offices as well as on the factory floor.

(The Foy and Gibson Ltd Collection, The University of Melbourne Archives)

While middle-class girls saw office work as a way of maintaining respectability and social status while earning a living, working-class girls were probably attracted to the work because it represented a step up (in social terms) from domestic service or factory work. For these girls the price of social advancement was high: like shop assistants, they were expected to maintain a high standard of dress and appearance. Turning up at the office each day in a 'fresh', light-coloured blouse and pressed skirt often meant daily washing and ironing on top of a day's work at the typewriter. There was also the cost of buying these clothes to consider, and the cost of keeping them clean and neat. Boarding houses often charged extra for the fuel they used in washing and ironing. Nor was this additional expense made up for by higher wages: like shop assistants, female clerical workers were not usually paid any more than factory workers.

(See Document 5.6.)

Nevertheless, girls continued to jostle for places at Australia's typewriters. By the 1930s they outnumbered men in commercial offices, mainly doing typing, stenography and filing. With the increasing use of machines for bookkeeping and calculating, women were beginning to move into the accounts area, performing work which had previously been the preserve of male

DOCUMENT 5.6

Dressed for the job?

(*The Australian Women's Weekly*, 9 December 1933)

A profusion of frills around the neck is quite out of order for the office as with continuous wear they lose their freshness and consequently their charm. Blouses also should be of the simplest design . . . silk blouses cannot be surpassed for office, but to be effective they must be well and plainly made . . . a blouse worn with a smart skirt and a pretty chip straw hat, trimmed with a band of dark petersham, makes a very becoming office attire.

(*Civil Service Journal*, September 1913, cited in G. Reekie, 'Female office workers in Western Australia, 1895–1920: the process of feminization and patterns of consciousness', in L. Layman (ed.), *op. cit.*, p. 16)

● How has the style of the ideal 'business girl' changed between 1913 and 1933?

DOCUMENT 5.7

Recruits for the office

(Punch, 25 May 1916)

(West Australian, 24 September 1913)

● Both these advertisements are for
Stott's Business College. What
similarities and differences are there in
the appeals they make?

Every girl in the world whether pauper or millionaire should be
taught a profession so that she could support herself if the
necessity ever arose . . . Some catastrophe is likely to befall any
girl no matter whom she marries. Misfortune, disease, death are
no respecters of persons, and many a young woman who has begun
her honeymoon in a palace has ended her days in a poorhouse.

accountants and clerks. During and after World War I they were
also employed in banks, as shorthand-typists, sorters and filers,
and operators of ledger-posting and adding machines. Compared
to other employers, the banks were slow to use female workers,
and it was unusual for them to employ female tellers before
World War II; the responsible and discreet work of handling
money and customers' accounts was considered more suitable for
male management trainees.

(See Document 5.7.)

DOCUMENT 5.8

Women in the Commonwealth public service

The principle of 'Equal Pay for Equal Work' does not apply in the Commonwealth Service. The general principle is that females should not be employed upon work which the Administration regards as male work, and vice versa.

Prior to about 1910 female Clerks and Telegraphists and Postmistresses were employed and received the same rates as male officers filling similar positions . . . There are no legal barriers to the advancement of women to the highest classified positions.

For approximately twenty-five years, however, females have not been admitted to the Third Division, to which are allotted the highest paid officers. Female Clerks and Post-mistresses already in the Service are eligible for advancement on the same conditions as males. One female clerk has advanced to the position of Assessor, Grade IV, Taxation Branch, and three Postmistresses have been promoted to Grade III post offices. In a short process of time, the Third Division of the Commonwealth Service, assuming the present policy remains, will be staffed only by males. Females are not now eligible as candidates for the Clerical Examinations.

Fourth Division positions are open to females, if designated as 'female' positions. The general principle is that males are ineligible for appointment to 'female' positions, and females are ineligible for appointment to 'male' positions. The Public Service Board determines whether a position is 'male' or 'female'. In the Fourth Division, therefore, there is no competition between males and females for advancement . . .

Employment of Married Women: Married women are not eligible for employment, either permanently or temporarily, in the Commonwealth Service, unless there are very special circumstances. In isolated cases, deserted wives with dependants in necessitous circumstances have been engaged as office cleaners.

(Muriel Heagney, *Are Women Taking Men's Jobs?*, Hilton & Veitch, Melbourne, 1935, pp. 79–83)

• What does this report reveal about the changing opportunities for women in the Commonwealth public service in the first three decades of the twentieth century?

Both the Commonwealth and state public service made considerable use of cheap female office labour in the first forty years of the twentieth century. However, as in the case of postal and telegraph offices and commercial offices, females were employed in certain types of work only and in some cases female clerks were explicitly excluded from administrative jobs which had potential for promotion. A Royal Commission into the Commonwealth Public Service in 1918 justified this division on the grounds that 'routine, monotonous, repetitive work seems to

This article reflects the often-observed trend for employers to engage juvenile workers on lower rates of pay instead of adults in order to reduce costs during difficult economic times.

(*Smith's Weekly*, 17 December 1932)

ADULT WOMEN ARE THE WORST OFF

Pin-Money Salaries

"**D**EPRESSION" has exiled from their billets in Sydney fully 6000 girls and women who had supported themselves as typists. Almost 4500 of these unemployed are highly trained adult women, with valuable office experience; and only about 1500 of the job-seekers are girls in their teens.

A Valued Servant—

Among 12,000 to 14,000 typists still employed, the tendency is to engage smart girls, not yet entitled to claim full adult wage. A permanent career in business is not offered to them.

Every wise business or professional man knows the real value of a competent typist and secretary. Her quality of loyalty is one of her finest attributes.

It is a serious loss to city economics, that thousands of women with splendid office training are drifting away into inferior forms of service.

suit women . . . they are usefully engaged in it as they release young men of initiative for other work'. The Commonwealth public service also prohibited the employment of married women, either permanently or temporarily.

(See Document 5.8.)

Female office work thus shared many features with female shop work—the respectable, 'white-collar' image, the low status

(Minutes of Victorian Branch of Federated Clothing and Allied Trades Union of Australia, 28 May 1923)

● This recommendation was the Clothing Trades Union's response to the Clerks Union, which urged other unions to grant their clerical staff equal pay regardless of sex. Did the increase given to Miss Gowland really represent equal pay for equal work?

DOCUMENT 5.9

The principle of equal pay

'The Executive [of the Clothing Trades Union] recommended that the salary of Miss Gowland be revised to £5 per week in order that the principle of equal pay may be put into effect . . . .' Mr Wallis explained that a male clerk had been hired at £5 a week and since Miss Gowland was the senior clerk it seemed she should get at least the minimum wage paid to a male 'in so doing the principle of equal pay would be recognised.'

compared to men and the limited promotional opportunities. Female clerks differed, however, in one major respect: they were not as passive as their sisters in the shops. On the contrary, female clerks were at times quite militant in their union campaigns for better wages and conditions and were among the earliest and most enthusiastic (if unsuccessful) agitators for equal pay for the sexes. Indeed, the author of the extract in Document 5.8, Muriel Heagney, who founded the Council of Action for Equal Pay in 1937, began her career as a clerk during World War I. She did not live to see the eventual success of her efforts in the 1970s. Meanwhile, professional women fought similar battles.

(See Document 5.9.)

Commonwealth Bank, accounts machines, 1926. These accounts machines were the precursors of today's computers. They were usually operated by females.

(*Bank Notes*, October 1926. LaTrobe Collection, State Library of Victoria)

Notes

Department stores and special detectives—Records of Paterson, Laing and Bruce Pty Ltd, ANU Archives of Business and Labour.

H. H. Richardson, *The Fortunes of Richard Mahony—Ultima Thule*, Heinemann, London, 1929, p. 283. Cited in Claire McCluskey, 'Women in the Victorian Post Office', in M. Bevege, M. James and C. Shute, *Worth Her Salt: Women at Work in Australia*, Hale & Iremonger, Sydney, 1982, p. 52.

'A woman who attended a small private boarding school'—Jan Carter, *Nothing to Spare: Recollections of Australian Pioneering Women*, Penguin, Ringwood, 1986, p. 41.

Muriel Heagney—Jean Bremner, 'In the cause of equality: Muriel Heagney and the position of women in the Depression', in M. Bevege, M. James and C. Shute (eds), *op. cit.*, pp. 286–98.

SUGGESTIONS FOR STUDY

For discussion

1 Do you think it would have been better to have worked in an office or a shop before World War II? Why?
2 Why do you think young men stopped learning to type once large numbers of women became typists?
3 Today, most offices use computers and word processors as well as typewriters. Who operate them?
4 Why did some jobs in offices come to be seen as female jobs and others as male jobs?
5 We saw how the public service formally discriminated against both single and married women before World War II. Does it still do so? What kinds of jobs do clerks employed in government departments do today? Are they routine or responsible, decision-making jobs? Are men or women employed in these jobs?

To write about

1 You are the manager of a big city department store in 1900. Prepare a report for your board of directors on how you propose to reduce the firm's labour costs. Remember that you have both sales and office staff to consider.
2 Now you are the secretary of the Shop Assistants and Office Workers Union. Prepare a report for your union members on how you expect the manager's proposals (in question 1) to affect them.
3 Compile a daily diary for a female shop assistant in a large department store in the 1920s. Note your reactions to your physical environment, your fellow workers and customers. Be sure to date your diary.

Community resources

The world of commerce

1 Make an appointment to interview one of the managers at a supermarket or large department store. Ask them about the different sorts of work performed by women and men. Which work do you think is more rewarding in terms of status, security and pay? Which offers any prospect of a satisfying career?
2 Which of the jobs in the store are mechanised and which are not? Is there a distinction between these mundane mechanised tasks and dealing with the public at large? Note the 'conversations' which take place between customers and the 'check-out staff'. Would service have been any more personalised in the past?
3 If you live in a suburb or town more than fifty years old, explore your local streetscape. Compare the fading names on shop pediments with those emblazoned across the windows of the store. Where you have found the oldest businesses, interview their workers or owners. Are they a family-run concern? If so, what role did women and children play in the day-to-day running of the store?
OR
3 If you live in a newer suburb or town, visit your local shopping centre. Make a note of the different types of shops in the centre and the kinds of service they provide to customers (i.e., self-service or individual attention). Which shops provide the most personal service and which the least? Can you explain the difference?
4 Can the shops you pass be classified in ethnic or gender terms? Which shops are likely to employ women? Which are run by Italians, Greeks or Vietnamese? How has this owner/employer pattern changed over time?

Museums

5 Visit your local museum. Which forms of technology presented there have made a significant impact on women's working lives?
6 Consider the museum's exhibits in the light of developments today. Is there any evidence that the mechanisation of certain tasks has led to women replacing men?

6 The Professions

Teaching

Colonial women from prosperous families had a different range of paid jobs from which to choose than did women from working-class families. Compared to Eleanor, who had barely two years' schooling, women who came from professional, business or landowning families were well educated. Although the education of young women usually placed great emphasis on 'feminine accomplishments' (such as music, painting, singing, dancing, modern languages and refined manners), subjects such as English language and literature, arithmetic, geography, history and Bible studies were considered just as important in the education of young women as they were to that of their brothers. The major aim of this type of schooling was to qualify young women for 'the thorough fulfilment of those important duties which fall to the lot of womanhood', as one Melbourne girls school expressed it. In other words, it hoped to make women more interesting and entertaining companions for men and better mothers in that they could pass on their learning to their children. It was certainly not intended as preparation for a lifelong career in business or the professions. Young women of the 'better classes' expected to stay at home with their mothers until they married a man who would keep them in idleness (or at least in unpaid domestic or charitable work) thereafter.

Women's lives did not always follow this ideal pattern. Family misfortune could mean that middle-class women, whether married, widowed or single, would be forced to provide for themselves and others. In such cases, their education could be turned into marketable skills. Had Eleanor Hargreaves come from such a background, she could have established a small school in her own home and charged her students fees. Such private establishments were the major form of schooling for 'young ladies' in the nineteenth century, and the numbers increased sharply after the 1850s when the newly rich gold rush generation sought ways to raise their daughters' manners to a level appropriate for their wealth.

A class in Queensland, circa 1902.
(Collection, John Oxley Library, Brisbane)

A class at Rosewood School, Queensland, circa ?1929.
(Collection, John Oxley Library, Brisbane)

Compare these two classes. What similarities and differences are there?

State School Teachers' Conference, Brisbane, June 1889. What does this sketch suggest about the role female teachers played within the teaching profession?

(*Boomerang*, 19 January 1889, p. 10)

Formal teacher training as we know it today, with special colleges and university courses, did not exist until the early twentieth century, so almost anyone could set up a school. For widows with children to support, the home-based school was particularly attractive as they could combine their paid work with their domestic responsibilities in the same way that a clothing outworker like Eleanor could. And like sewing, teaching was considered a natural extension of women's traditional role of caring for children in a family environment.

A school of one's own was not the only option for women who could teach. Governessing was a popular occupation for single women who were employed by individual families to care for and educate their children. The more fortunate found congenial employment and homes with families of similar social standing.

The daughter of Perth's Anglican Archbishop, for instance, worked for a time as governess to the children of Western Australia's Governor. She was unusual in that her father believed in education for women and had sent her to Cambridge University. It was this characteristic, however, which marked her as a member of the social elite and therefore a suitable person to share the Governor's household. As she said:

In those days there were governesses and governesses: I was also a lady to look after the governor's children and it was easier for me than for others. The things the girls were invited to, I probably would have gone to anyway.

But as she also noted, one did not need a Cambridge degree to be an ordinary governess. 'People very often got a governess to look after the children, irrespective of their education'. A normal middle-class schooling was sufficient. However, governessing was not something a mother could do easily, as she had her own children to care for. As Document 6.1 notes, it was not a well-paid occupation.

DOCUMENT 6.1

A governess's wages

INSOLENT PLUTOCRACY.

MISTRESS (engaging cook): "And what about wages; shall we say fifteen shillings?"

COOK: "Fifteen shillings! What do you take me for; is it a poor governess yer think yer engaging?"

(*Bulletin*, 28 April 1900)

With the emergence of compulsory education in most colonies in the 1870s, there were opportunities for women to teach. Both married and single women were employed by the colonial governments to teach the children of the working class and the poorer sections of the middle class. Often, whole families—father, mother, sons and daughters—would teach at the same school. These teachers were trained on-the-job, like apprentices. Senior students were promoted to pupil–teachers, or monitors, and helped the experienced teacher until they could pass the exams and be appointed to teaching jobs of their own. This system allowed some people from poorer backgrounds to move out of the working class, so that teaching was an important avenue for social mobility as well as an employer of middle-class women. The main drawback with this kind of work was that there were always more women seeking positions than there were vacancies, and unless one had connections with the local school boards or education department authorities, obtaining a job could be very difficult. (See Document 6.2.)

(*Memories of Alice Henry*, edited by Nettie Palmer, Melbourne, 1944, p. 8)

• What do Alice Henry's memoirs tell us about the reasons some women did, or did not, become teachers?

DOCUMENT 6.2

'Not cut out for teaching'

In a vague way I expected that of course I'd marry. But that was some day, and boys and young men were very scarce in my home circle. But it was quite certain that I was to earn my living. There was rather an idea with both our parents that their children should rise in station; and there was nothing for me but teaching and very little opportunity of qualifying for that. So I was lucky to be accepted as a pupil teacher in Mr. Budd's College. But I was never cut out for a regular teacher. To teach a class for one year was interesting; to have to go back and start all over again with another class was, from my view of self-development, the most futile performance. An illness of my own, followed by a long illness of my father, stopped any regular career of that sort.

Another problem for female teachers was the changing attitude to the employment of married women. The Victorian Education Department dismissed almost all its married female teachers during the depression of the 1890s. New South Wales teachers suffered a similar fate during the depression of the 1930s.

In general, however, opportunities for women in teaching expanded in the fifty years before the outbreak of World War II in 1939. Kindergartens opened in urban centres in the 1890s, providing work which was considered particularly suitable for women. The expansion of state secondary education from the turn of the century also opened up new opportunities for teachers of both sexes, and special domestic science training centres were staffed almost entirely by women.

Despite expanding opportunities for women in teaching, women did not enter the education system on equal terms with men. The Victorian situation is representative. Women's salaries were fixed at about four-fifths those paid to men doing similar work, and this proportion fell even lower in the 1890s when the

DOCUMENT 6.3

A man's job

For your information I will state the reasons why I regard this position as being essentially one that requires a man.

The field of post-primary education presents the most difficult problems in the whole educational field at the present time. For the first time in our history, education for all beyond the primary stage is being provided, and it is essential in the organization of this field that the education should be adapted to the future needs of adolescent boys and girls. So far as girls are concerned the problem is much simpler than that presented by the needs of the boys. Some girls enter into wage earning occupations but even of these the great majority will become housewives and drop out of these occupations in a few years. The boys, on the other hand, have to start on their life's work, and the educational system should be directed to fitting them for their future vocation in the best possible way. Their needs are not nearly covered by the relatively simple curriculum that is necessary for girls. Varying types of courses including an increasing amount of practical and pre-vocational work must be provided, and I hold strongly that only a man with the full knowledge of modern conditions and of the educational needs of boys can adequately fill such a position. On the administrative side the Chief Inspector has to interview parents and councils, discuss all manner of details, even those dealing with sanitary arrangements, holding inquiries into complaints often involving sex matters, and these duties, I am satisfied a woman should not be called upon to undertake.

(Minute prepared by the Director of Education, Victoria, 2 August 1928, from K. Daniels and M. Murnane (eds), *Uphill All the Way: A Documentary History of Women: Australia*, University of Queensland Press, St Lucia, 1980, pp. 250–1)

• Do you think these objections to a female Chief Inspector of Schools are valid?

wages of female teachers were cut much more severely than those of males. Women also had fewer opportunities for promotion: they could only be principals of one-teacher schools, schools for the handicapped or girls schools. Married women could not apply for promotion. Women also faced discrimination in applying for administrative jobs within the growing Victorian Department of Education. The case of Julia Flynn demonstrates the continuing reluctance of many men to accept women in positions of authority over the opposite sex.

Julia Flynn: 'Teacher at the top'

Compared to the anonymous thousands of women who worked as teachers for Victoria's Education Department over the last hundred years or so, Julia Flynn stands out as a well-known and controversial person. Her fame is a result of the fact that she was associated with so many firsts in teaching: she was one of the first women to move from primary to secondary teaching; the first woman to be appointed an inspector of schools; the first woman to become Assistant Chief Inspector; and the first woman Chief Inspector. In addition, her appointment to such senior positions became the focus for arguments between men and women about the appropriate role for women within the Education Department.

Julia began her fifty-year career in 1893 after matriculating at Presbyterian Ladies College at the young age of fifteen. She completed the usual course of on-the-job teacher training as a monitor and pupil-teacher in 1897 and two years later became one of the first group of students to attend the newly reopened Melbourne Teachers' College (which had closed during the depression). She was awarded her Trained Teachers' Certificate in 1900 and was selected to extend her training at the University of Melbourne. For the next fourteen years she taught at various primary and secondary schools around Melbourne and Victorian country towns, at the same time adding to her qualifications by part-time study. In 1914 she was appointed to one of the newly created positions of inspector of secondary schools. There were only two such inspectors in Victoria. The other inspector was a man. Julia Flynn received four-fifths of the salary paid to her male colleague.

In 1928 the position of Assistant Chief Inspector became vacant but was advertised with the male rate of pay, implying that applications from women were not welcome. Flynn successfully protested to the Minister of Education about this obvious discrimination and was subsequently appointed to the job, again at four-fifths the male rate of pay. Shortly after taking up the Assistant Chief Inspectorship, the Chief Inspector's job became vacant and she was made Acting Chief Inspector in June 1928.

In July 1928 the Chief Inspectorship was advertised, and as she was already doing this job Julia Flynn believed she would be the most suitable candidate. However, the advertisement called specifically for male applications only. This decision had been made by the male Director of Education, Martin Hansen, who argued that a woman could not do the work.

(See Document 6.3.)

His decision caused an outcry from women's groups and led to a public debate in the press and in the Victorian parliament. Hansen was forced to back down, and Flynn applied. Again she faced discrimination as her application was passed over and a more junior male appointed. She immediately appealed to the Public Service Commissioner who supported her protest. Her victory was shortlived; when her period of probation expired the Director refused to recommend her as the permanent Chief Inspector. Despite public uproar, Hansen remained firm and she resumed her position as Assistant Chief.

When the man appointed in her stead was promoted to Director of Education in 1936, Julia Flynn again became Chief Inspector. But this time there was no fuss, and she remained in the position until her retirement in 1943. She never, however, received the same salary as her male predecessor nor did she have the opportunity he had of rising to the very highest post in the Education Department.

Like Julia Flynn, many other women teachers did not passively accept substandard pay, conditions and opportunities, and fought to change the system. Unlike nurses, who worked in an all-female area, female teachers were constantly confronted with the devaluation of their services. They worked alongside men who were no better trained or qualified and no more competent, yet who received better pay and greater opportunities. Their relatively high level of education seems to have made them more critical of the society in which they lived and willing to work for change. Teachers were prominent in the campaign for votes for women, and several (for example, Ellen Mulcahy and Florence Johnson) devoted their lives to wider feminist causes such as the organisation of women's trade unions and campaigns to improve the housing of the poor. Since many teachers came from working-class homes themselves, trade union principles were not as foreign to them as they were to most nurses.

Much of Julia Flynn's success, limited though it was by her sex, rested on the fact that she was single and without dependants. It would have been much harder for her to have gained those 'unsurpassed qualifications' had she been trying to juggle domestic responsibilities as well as a full-time job and part-time study. Had she been a married woman she could not have been appointed to the full-time permanent staff in the Victorian public service. Dr Vera Scantlebury Brown, who became Director of Infant Welfare in the 1930s, could only fill this position as a married woman because she agreed to work full-time yet accept an official appointment (and pay) as part-time. Nor would she have attracted the same degree of support from single female teachers, many of whom shared the hostility of most men to working wives. Julia Flynn's case shows the real opportunities open to women of ability in teaching in the first half of the twentieth century, but it also reveals the continuing discrimination against them because of their sex.

University teaching and research

Although women were admitted as students at Australian universities from the 1880s, they rarely rose above the most junior ranks of the academic staff before the 1970s. It was not just that universities discriminated, either deliberately or unconsciously, against female academics. Probably more important was the difficulty of combining a full-time university job with the domestic responsibilities which still fell to women. This not only posed practical problems for the women who tried to do both, but also deterred universities from employing anyone who would have to be a 'superwoman'. As late as 1968, the University of Western Australia refused to appoint married women to its permanent staff; Document 6.4 suggests one reason why they were seen as a problem. Certainly, university authorities have only recently begun to accept new employment arrangements designed to ease the double burden on women academics.

DOCUMENT 6.4

Married women as academics

25th June, 1968.

Mrs. E. Highet,
Hon. Secretary, Western Australian
    Association of University Women,
5 Graham Court,
COTTESLOE.   W.A. 6011.

Dear Mrs. Highet,

Thank you for your letter of the 17th June, 1968. We are slowly hammering out our policy on the employment of married women and I shall be glad to let you know what is finally decided.

You may possibly appreciate the fact that in the University, academics are employed not from 9.00 a.m. to 5.00 p.m. but are required to devote their whole time and attention to teaching and research. As you can probably imagine, this creates somewhat of a problem for the young married woman unless she is fortunate enough to be able to ensure continuously the services of a competent housekeeper and nurse.

With kindest regards,

Yours sincerely,

Stanley Prescott
Vice-Chancellor.

(Patricia Crawford and Myrna Tonkinson, *The Missing Chapters,* Centre for West Australian History, University of Western Australia, Document 5, 1988)

● Patricia Crawford and Myrna Tonkinson, in their book *The Missing Chapters*, tell of the battle women academics had to obtain access to permanent university appointments at the University of Western Australia. This letter shows one response of the authorities to their appeal. Do you think the Vice-Chancellor's objection to married women a valid one? What other possible strategies are there for mothers who wish also to have academic careers?

Nursing

Nursing, like teaching, was another 'female' career which developed rapidly from the late nineteenth century. Before the 1880s, nursing was usually performed by the roughest class of domestic servant; a respectable girl of good family would no more choose it as a career than she would think of becoming a street prostitute. All this changed with the success of the English nurse Florence Nightingale in raising the status of nursing to a ladylike occupation. Her ideas were applied in all the major Australian cities in the 1870s, 1880s and 1890s.

The prospect of a respectable alternative to staying at home proved enormously attractive to Australian women from families who could afford the financial burden of partially supporting their daughters during the three- or four-year training period. (Trainee nurses were paid only a few shillings a week in their first year, increasing to a mere ten shillings by the third year.) Many were disappointed, as strict entry requirements applied to the selection of trainees. One nurse, the daughter of a moderately prosperous Western Australian farmer, recalled the appeal nursing held for her, and also its exclusiveness:

This cartoon depicts the common belief that nursing offered a woman good marriage prospects, if not to a male doctor then to a well-off patient.

(*Bulletin*, 3 October 1912)

Every year there is an increase in the **number of girls who are attracted to the nursing profession.** Nursing is the finest possible occupation for the girl who wants intellectual interests but the nurse has a long and difficult road to travel before she can even dream of possessing a banking account.—Melb. paper.

Nonsence ! She has only to be nice to some rich convalescent and the bank a/c is assured.

Nursing was my ambition. I wanted to look after people. Nursing was considered a good thing. You were doing something for someone not able to help themselves . . . Nurses were expected to bring a letter of introduction from three prominent people, including a minister . . . I know the girls I went in with were, looking back on them, very respectable people. I think they came from those kinds of families.

A home away from home—Brisbane Children's Hospital. In the romanticised environment of a private children's hospital, nurses took the place of absent mothers. A mother's love was considered no match for professional training.

(*Boomerang*, 18 September 1888, p. 18)

Nursing also held attractions for working-class women in that it seemed to offer them an increase in social status and better marriage prospects. But few labourers' daughters were able to realise an ambition to become a nurse. The same exclusiveness which raised the status of nursing to a genteel profession also prevented most working-class women from undertaking training. The preference of training hospitals for recruits aged between twenty and thirty years further limited access to the profession.

Those who were accepted into the ranks of trainee nurses faced a life of extremely hard work and considerable risk. Most nurses worked at least twelve hours a day, doing heavy and dirty manual work which contrasted sharply with the genteel image they projected. Nurses were required to live in the hospitals during training in quarters which were often uncomfortable and vermin-infested. Their lives, both on and off duty, were carefully supervised so as to avoid behaviour which would then have been considered immoral. As well, nurses were constantly exposed to the danger of catching their patients' diseases. Conditions were at their worst on the newly established Western Australian goldfields, where each summer typhoid and diphtheria epidemics raged through the townships. Nurse Jenkins, who arrived in Kalgoorlie late in 1895, described conditions in the government hospital where she worked:

Beds in the tents lay so close together it was just possible to squeeze between them. As soon as a patient began to improve he was placed on a mattress on the floor, often stepping over patients to get from one to another. For months I never worked less than 12 hours a day and often 14 or 15 . . .

When the staff increased, Nurse Jenkins was given one day off a month, but by the time her day off came she was too exhausted to do anything but lie in bed: 'I was invariably stricken with a

'Ministering Angels'—Nursing Sisters of St John of God Hospital, Kalgoorlie, with Dr Burton, 1911. Religious orders attracted many women to serve God and their fellows as a lifelong vocation. While most women in religious vocations were engaged in teaching, those shown here worked in a Catholic hospital.

(Golden Mile Museum 1202, Kalgoorlie)

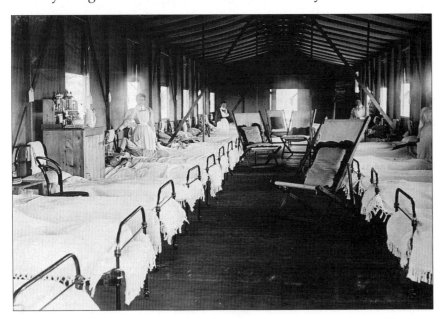

No. 9 Ward, Coolgardie Hospital, circa 1897. The crowded conditions in this makeshift goldfields' hospital compare unfavourably with the comfortable, homely wards in the Brisbane Children's Hospital (p. 116.

(Battye Library, 66378P)

General Hospital, Hobart. How does this nineteenth-century ward compare with most modern hospital surroundings?

(Joan C. Brown, *'Poverty is not a Crime': The Development of Social Services in Tasmania 1803–1900*, Tasmanian Historical Research Association, Hobart, 1972, p. 104)

nervous headache on that day, I believe it was sheer reaction'. It did not help that when on night duty she had to try to sleep during the day in a small tent with temperatures up to 45 °C. Not surprisingly over half the hospital's staff, including the matron and doctor, were stricken with typhoid before the summer was over.

Even in the more established colonial cities such as Melbourne, conditions were harsh. Marie Magill, who started training at Melbourne's Alfred Hospital in 1890, found she was expected to start her day at 5.30 a.m. and frequently worked to 8.30 p.m. or even later. She slept in a tent with eleven other nurses next to the typhoid ward. Of these eleven nurses, six contracted typhoid, four seriously (one of whom died).

Nor was the pay of the qualified nurse any compensation for her discomfort. The most fortunate could expect a mere one hundred pounds per year in the early twentieth century, 'an income in inverse proportion to the hours worked, and the skill required in her calling, and an income less than that paid to the cook of a third-class hotel or a girl on the telephone exchange'.

Despite these appalling conditions, few nurses complained or attempted to improve the circumstances of nurses in general. Those who could not cope with the rigours of the life simply left, as did Nurse Magill, who returned to her former occupation of governess. A minority were able to establish their own private

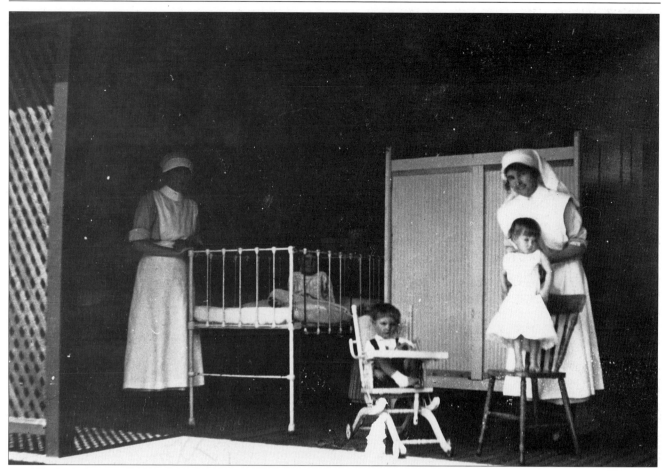

hospitals where they acted as matrons and employed other women to do the heavier, more menial tasks. But the ideal of self-sacrifice, dedication and unquestioning acceptance of authority upon which the occupation's claims to professional and genteel status rested, prevented nurses from engaging in collective bargaining for shorter hours and improved wages and conditions. Trade unions were considered both unladylike and unprofessional.

Not all women who earnt their living at nursing worked within the hospital system. Some worked privately, tending patients in their homes. For them, hours, conditions and pay were little better or even worse than those in hospitals. Many private nurses specialised in midwifery, since before the 1930s babies were usually delivered at home by midwives. In the nineteenth century, the qualifications and expertise of these women varied greatly, but the high demand for their services in preference to more expensive (and not necessarily more competent) doctors ensured that this was one field in which women with some experience could obtain an independent income.

In the early twentieth century, midwifery underwent much more dramatic change than regular nursing. This was largely caused by the determination of nurses and doctors to professionalise midwifery—to ensure that only formally trained and registered midwives (or doctors) attended women in childbirth. While in the long term this may have raised the status

Children's Ward, Fremantle, circa 1920, with Sister Leo and Nurse Arnold. The stark clinical environment of this 1920s children's ward contrasts sharply with the homely surrounding of the Brisbane Children's Hospital ward (p. 116). It is also very different to the bright and interesting wards provided by most children's hospitals in the 1990s. Why do you think styles in hospital furnishing have changed in this way?

(Battye Library)

of midwives, in the short term it meant that many experienced, and competent women were prevented from earning a living by delivering babies; many considered themselves too old or ill-educated to pass the exams, while others could not afford the registration fee. And while registration limited the numbers legally entitled to practice midwifery, the trend towards hospital births under medical supervision in the 1920s and 1930s, and the general fall in the birth rate from the 1880s, reduced the demand for midwives' services.

General nurses, on the other hand, experienced a continual increase in demand for their services as hospitals became more acceptable places for the treatment of the ill as well as the dying. The extension of Florence Nightingale's system of nursing in the twentieth century, and the heroic role played by nurses during World War I (1914–1918), secured the respectable status of the profession. The sewering of most major towns and cities in the years prior to World War II, and greater awareness of public health in general, also reduced the risks of nurses catching diseases such as typhoid. Hospital buildings and nurses' quarters also became more substantial and hence more comfortable places in which to live and work. However, long hours of work and low rates of pay continued; not until the late 1930s did the nursing profession show any interest in raising its working conditions to levels achieved by many industrial workers forty years earlier. The effect this had on women's ability to make a lifelong career in nursing is well illustrated by the case of Ruth Dunlop. Her case also shows that while some avenues were closing for nurses, others were opening up.

Ruth Dunlop: Nurse, midwife, policewoman

Ruth Dunlop (nee Gloster) was born in Seymour, Victoria, in 1883, the eleventh child of a local draper and his wife. Like many Victorians, they were driven by the economic depression of the 1890s to try their luck on the Western Australian goldfields. Ruth trained at the Coolgardie and Kalgoorlie hospitals and completed her general certificate in 1909. She moved with her family to Perth and commenced work nursing people privately in their own homes. In April 1914 she married J. Robert Dunlop, a branch manager for Burns, Philp and Company. Shortly after their marriage they moved to Sydney where two children were born, a son in 1915 and a daughter the following year. When baby Margaret was less than two years old, her father died from a congenital heart disorder. Ruth was determined to provide for her children herself, rather than place them in an orphanage, but realised that this was impossible on an ordinary nurse's wages. With the financial help of her sister, she was able to have a woman care for her children while she completed her midwifery training.

After completing the course, Ruth returned to Perth in 1920 but found that midwifery was not such a good career for someone in her circumstances. The hours were too long and uncertain and the income too irregular at a time when more women were having their babies in hospital rather than at home. In 1921 she decided to abandon this work and applied instead to become a policewoman, which offered better wages and more regular hours.

Policewomen had first been appointed in Australia during World War I (1914–18). It was hoped that women police could deter individuals from falling into a life of prostitution or crime by the exercise of a firm 'motherly' influence. The Western Australian Commissioner of Police sought a special sort of woman for his force: she had to be of 'strong moral character' and a qualified nursing sister. Ruth satisfied both requirements, and so began a career which was to last until her retirement from paid work in 1943.

During the decade following 1921, Woman Police Constable Dunlop was able to survive in rented premises in Fremantle and Perth, where a network of family and friends helped out with child-care. Fellow police officers also helped, the local sergeant and his wife providing lunch for the children when they attended school near the police station. When all else failed, Ruth took Margaret and Peter to work with her and employed a 'girl' to stay with them and feed them in the policewomen's office above the lockup. In this way she was able to make ends meet until her children were old enough to take care of themselves.

The 'women's police'

Western Australian policewomen at this time were mainly concerned with the welfare of women and children. They did not wear uniforms, nor did they participate in the same range of duties as policemen. Their status in the force reflected the low value given to work with women and children. Despite the fact that policewomen were more highly qualified than most male recruits (since they had to be registered nurses), women could not rise above the rank of constable. They were not regarded as 'real' police by their male colleagues, nor accepted as full members of the police union until the 1960s.

Journalism

Writing and producing magazines and newspapers offered some opportunities to women with the appropriate skills, although the number of positions open to them and the type of work they could

A female broadcaster, 1930s. The advent of radio broadcasting opened up new opportunities for both male and female journalists. But men and women did not participate in the new medium in the same ways. Ask an older member of your family or community about the different sorts of programs presented by men and women before World War II.

(*Australian Women's Diary*, Doubleday, Sydney, 1989)

do were very limited. In 1891, for instance, there were only twenty-eight women recorded at the Victorian Census as 'journalist or author', compared to 506 men. Most of these women were employed to write for women's magazines or to prepare special women's columns for general newspapers: they were much more likely to be writing the social notes than articles on politics, commerce or sport. Occasionally, a woman of extraordinary determination and talent could break into the male realm of political journalism. For example, Alice Henry, who went on to become a distinguished union organiser in the United States, began her career as a freelance journalist in Melbourne in the 1880s. Other enterprising women struck out on their own and produced journals. Louisa Lawson, a prominent Sydney feminist and mother of Henry Lawson, started producing *Dawn* in 1888. This journal, which came out monthly until 1905, was devoted to feminist concerns and employed women to set the type as well as to write the articles.

(See Document 6.5.)

DOCUMENT 6.5

First journalistic experience

I well remember my feeling of satisfaction when an original article of mine, based on personal experience, advocating the use of coke as a fuel, was published in November 1884. Some time after this I secured a position on the staff of *The Australasian*. My beginnings in journalism were indeed humble. I started at the bottom of the ladder, society reporting, furnishing cookery recipes, especially American recipes gleaned from the wife of an American dentist settled in Melbourne, all of them, of course, modestly under a nom de plume, Pomona. Mason jars, thus recommended, were christened 'Pomona Jars'.

(*Memoirs of Alice Henry*, edited by Nettie Palmer, 1944, p. 13)

● Do you think that 'starting at the bottom' for a male journalist would have involved the same tasks as those assigned this woman?

Medicine

Medicine was another professional occupation which gradually opened its doors to women over the period from approximately 1880 to 1940. Indeed, Alice Henry had originally planned to become a doctor, but the University of Melbourne did not accept female medical students until 1887. Although a trickle of female graduates appeared each year after 1891, it was a very demanding career for a woman to choose. For a start, it was considered 'a funny thing for a girl to want to do', so the female doctor was looked on with curiosity if not open hostility. Then there was the problem of fees, which were prohibitive to all but the children of well-off families or those fortunate enough to win a university scholarship. Young women who survived the coarse jokes of lecturers and male students during university then faced discrimination in being assigned to hospitals for resident training. Some hospitals refused to take female graduates until the 1920s, and female residents were not allowed to work in casualty where some of the most valuable experience was to be gained. Dr Kate Campbell recalls the treatment received by herself and her fellows in the early 1920s:

At the end of our course, there was fierce competition for residentships . . . The Alfred Hospital would not take girls at all, even the brightest, and always the same excuse if any of the women protested: 'We haven't any toilet arrangements!' We were admitted to the Melbourne, but given 'accidentally' and not as a policy, all the dirty work . . . The men were assigned to all the leading lights [and] the male doctors in casualty would choose their own male friends to receive the most interesting and important cases by sending them to their friends' wards.

It was this official and unofficial discrimination against female doctors which prompted a group of twelve Melbourne women to

Medical Theatre, University of Adelaide, 1906. In the intensely masculine world of the medical school, the few female students sit together for mutual support.

(*Critic*, in Helen Jones, *In Her Own Name: Women in South Australian History,* Wakefield Press, Adelaide, 1986, p. 216)

Psychology Class, University of Adelaide, 1906. Women found it easier to participate in the newer paramedical professions such as psychology than in the more traditional areas of surgery and physical medicine.

(*Critic*, in Helen Jones, *op. cit.*)

found their own hospital in 1896. At the Queen Victoria Hospital, women could be treated by women doctors. Some doctors attribute the improved status and conditions for women doctors in the twentieth century largely to the training provided at this hospital.

(See Document 6.6.)

After residency (the period of compulsory hospital work required to complete a medical qualification), there was the exhausting life of the general practitioner to look forward to:

DOCUMENT 6.6

A women's hospital

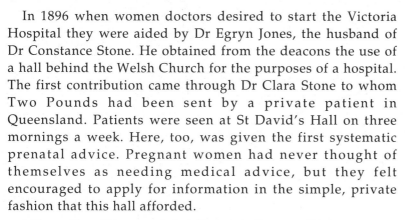

In 1896 when women doctors desired to start the Victoria Hospital they were aided by Dr Egryn Jones, the husband of Dr Constance Stone. He obtained from the deacons the use of a hall behind the Welsh Church for the purposes of a hospital. The first contribution came through Dr Clara Stone to whom Two Pounds had been sent by a private patient in Queensland. Patients were seen at St David's Hall on three mornings a week. Here, too, was given the first systematic prenatal advice. Pregnant women had never thought of themselves as needing medical advice, but they felt encouraged to apply for information in the simple, private fashion that this hall afforded.

When the Diamond Jubilee of Queen Victoria was celebrated, Her Majesty expressed the desire that the funds raised for the occasion should be spent on the welfare of women and children. By June 22nd there was raised £3162/11/9 through a shilling fund. In July 1899 the Queen Victoria Hospital was opened with an out-patients' department, a dispensary and an operating theatre. To begin with, there were only eight beds. Mr Bristow was the first dispenser, but as soon as a woman dispenser was available her services were secured. This happened to be Miss Wollen, afterwards my sister-in-law, Mrs Alfred Henry. She was a gold medallist of the College of Pharmacy, Melbourne, and retained this position until September 1905. She then held a similar position in Launceston General Hospital until her marriage in 1907.

From these small beginnings the work has steadily increased until to-day there are over 180 in-patients every day and over a thousand out-patients every week, with every department and every service at the highest standard of equipment.

(*Memoirs of Alice Henry*, edited by Nettie Palmer, Melbourne, 1944, p. 19)

● The Queen Victoria Hospital provided work for many female doctors. What other female health professionals did it employ?

There was no social life, no rest in bed. You might have a confinement at night, get to bed for half an hour, and an hour later be called out again. (Kate Campbell)

Such a life was suitable only for a single woman or a married woman who had the kind of support usually given to male doctors by their wives:

A married woman in those days could not have maintained a practice and raised a family without a 'stand-in'. Most of the women doctors I knew did not marry. If they married and did not have any children they could practise. The few with children who did practise had a mother or aunt who took their place in the family. The married women often took sessional jobs, but didn't work full time. (Kate Campbell)

DOCUMENT 6.7

A clever lady doctor

Mrs. Dr. Thymol, of 17 Newtown-road, Darlington, Sydney, is causing quite a sensation by some of the marvellous cures in apparently incurable cases of St. Vitus' Dance, Eye, Ear, and Glandular and Hip Diseases in Children. Should you be suffering with Epilepsy, or any nervous complaints, Ulcers, Female Exhaustion, or Loss of Energy, you should consult her. All ladies suffering with complaints, which, from motives of modesty, they would not consult a doctor about, should avail themselves of the assistance and advice of this Diplomaed Lady Practitioner, whose acknowledged skill, combined with strictest secrecy and firmest confidence, first meets the demand of those sufferers of her sex, who have hitherto been obliged to lay their complaints before male doctors. —Advt.

(*Illawarra Mercury*, 23 August 1890)

• What does this advertisement say about the type of patients 'Mrs. Dr. Thymol' treats and why they might choose her as their medical practitioner?

Dr Vera Scantlebury Brown is one such case. She was able to continue her distinguished career as Director of Infant Welfare in Victoria after the birth of her two children only by employing a mothercraft nurse and a housekeeper to help out with 'her' domestic duties.

Hostility from men in the profession and the difficulties of balancing professional and domestic demands meant that most women doctors tended to work in a limited range of medical jobs. Work with women and children was considered particularly suitable for them, and the public service offered more reasonable working hours than private practice. Not surprisingly, then, a disproportionate number found their way into the offices of the public health services, holding appointments as school medical officers and health inspectors as well as working in government departments set up after World War I to look after infant and maternal welfare. Female doctors were also found working part-time in general practices, but almost never in the exclusive consulting rooms of specialist surgeons or physicians. Female dentists had similar experiences, and were disproportionately employed in school dental services.
(See Document 6.7.)

Law

Women were able to become lawyers early in the twentieth century, the first, Florence Greig, graduating from the University of Melbourne in 1903. Florence Greig was also the first woman admitted to the Victorian Bar (that is, she became a barrister), but a special amendment to the *Legal Profession Practice Act* had to be passed to allow her to do so. This Act was commonly known as the 'Flos Greig Enabling Bill' by her colleagues. Few women, however, followed in her footsteps, most female law graduates earning their livings among the less glamorous paperwork of a solicitor's office.

Social work

Social work (along with physiotherapy) was a new profession which, from the outset, attracted and accepted female members. Modern social work, with its emphasis on sustained contact between the social worker and the client (casework), had its origins in the philanthropic work directed by the Charity Organisation Society in the 1890s. Although colonial social workers were usually middle-class women performing voluntary work, by the mid-1890s charitable societies were also employing paid agents to investigate and report on cases in order to assess

Lesbia Keogh, graduation from Melbourne University, 1916. A few determined and resourceful women took teaching jobs to help pay for a university education. Lesbia graduated with a law degree. She is better known as the poet and novelist Lesbia Harford.

(State Library of Victoria)

> Jessie Brookes was one of the first students to complete the Diploma of Social Work at the University of Melbourne in 1936. Like the 'ladies bountiful' of the nineteenth century who visited the poor in their spare time, Jessie came from a privileged background. Her first job as a social worker was with the Victorian Crippled Children's Society. During the poliomyelitis epidemic of 1938 she organised the 'Polio Aunts', a support group for parents who had to teach children at home. (The regular schools were closed to try to prevent the spread of the disease.) Parents of handicapped children, Jessie believed, found this time particularly trying and her Polio Aunts were there to give these parents a helping hand.

their eligibility for benefits. This practice increased in the early twentieth century as various hospitals, businesses and government departments employed people especially to look after the welfare of the people with whom they dealt. By the 1920s and 1930s, the occupation of social worker was recognised as a semi-profession, requiring tertiary qualifications.

Jessie Brookes obviously had a very practical streak, as she later developed a thriving nappy-wash business. Other women sought their livings in what were considered to be higher pursuits in the world of literature, music, art and drama. They are the focus of Chapter 7.

Notes

'one Melbourne girls school'—Vieusseux Ladies' College, *Prospectus*, 1862, quoted in Marjorie Theobald, 'Julie Vieusseux: the lady principal', in M. Lake and F. Kelly (eds), *Double Time, Women in Victoria 150 Years*, Penguin, Ringwood, 1985, p. 81.

The daughter of Perth's Anglican Bishop—Jan Carter, *Nothing to Spare: Recollections of Australian Pioneering Women*, Penguin, Ringwood, 1986, p. 207.

Vera Scantlebury Brown—Kerreen Reiger, 'Vera Scantlebury Brown: professional mother', in M. Lake and F. Kelly (eds), *op. cit.*, pp. 288–96.

'one nurse'—Jan Carter, *op. cit.*, p. 141.

Nurse Jenkins—Norma King, *The Daughters of Midas: Pioneer Women on the Eastern Goldfields*, Hesperian Press, Perth, 1988, p. 39.

Marie Magill—Monica MacKay, 'Marie Magill, nurse: not such a brilliant career', in M. Lake and F. Kelly (eds), *op. cit.*, p. 136.

'an income in inverse proportion . . .'—'What is to become of the Australian nurse?', editorial, *Australasian Nurses' Journal*, August 1913, pp. 253–4. Cited in Glenda Law, '"I never liked trade unionism": the development of the Royal Australian Nursing Federation, Queensland Branch, 1904–1945', in E. Windschuttle (ed.), *Women, Class and History*, Fontana/Collins, Melbourne, 1980, p. 197.

Ruth Dunlop—Leonie Biggins, 'One of God's police? Policewoman Ruth Dunlop', in R. Frances and B. Scates (eds), *The Murdoch Ethos: Essays in Honour of Foundation Professor Geoffrey Bolton*, Murdoch University, WA, 1989, pp. 155–71.

Alice Henry—Nettie Palmer (ed.), *The Memoirs of Alice Henry*, Melbourne, 1944.

Louisa Lawson—E. Fry (ed.), *Rebels and Radicals*, George Allen & Unwin, Sydney, 1983.

'a funny thing for girls to want to do' (Kate Campbell)—'A medical life', in P. Grimshaw and L. Strahan (eds), *The Half-Open Door*, Hale & Iremonger, Sydney, 1982, p. 161.

Florence Greig—*Australian Working Women's Diary*, Doubleday, Sydney, 1988.

Jessie Brookes—Marjorie Tipping, 'Jessie Clarke: founder of Nappie Wash', in M. Lake and F. Kelly (eds), *op. cit.*, pp. 408–14.

SUGGESTIONS FOR STUDY

For discussion

1 What kind of training do you need today to become:
   a a kindergarten teacher?
   b a primary school teacher?
   c a secondary school teacher?
   d a lecturer at a college of advanced education or a university?

2 Why do so many women still choose teaching as a career?

3 Couples where both partners are teachers are the most likely occupational group to experiment with role-reversal and role-sharing arrangements (i.e., the woman earns while the man cares for the children/home; both man and woman work part-time or full-time in paid work and share parenting/housework). Why does this career lend itself so well to such alternatives?

4 How does the system of nurse training before World War II compare to that offered to today's nursing recruits?

5 More men become nurses today than ever before. How do you think this will influence nursing as a profession?

6 Has it become easier for women to succeed in journalism? What effect do you think television has had on journalism as a career for women?

7 What do the professions of teaching, nursing, medicine and social work have in common? Why do you think women seem to be more attracted to these than professions like engineering and the physical sciences?

To write about

1 Imagine you are an unmarried female schoolteacher reaching retirement in 1939. Write a speech you are to deliver at a farewell dinner in your honour given by your fellow teachers. Talk about the changes you have seen in the teaching profession during your forty-year career.

2 You are a reporter for a women's magazine in 1890. Write a report on the various careers in health-care open to women.

3 Write a similar report, this time dated 1930.

4 Write a women's column for a local newspaper in the 1930s. Discuss the issues you feel are of the most importance to women.

Community resources
People and professions

1 Survey the teachers at your school to determine who teaches which subjects and who has the most responsible jobs. Prepare two lists, one showing all the subjects taught in your school and the number and sex of the teachers involved, the other showing the various levels in the school teaching hierarchy (e.g., principal, deputy principal, series teacher, coordinator, class teacher) and the number and sex of teachers in each category. What conclusions can you draw from your survey? How do you account for any gender bias?

2 Extend your vocational hierarchy to include other areas of the teaching profession. Compare the pay and conditions of:
   a a kindergarten teacher,
   b a primary school teacher,
   c a secondary school teacher and
   d a lecturer at a college of advanced education or a university. Have these conditions changed over time? Why?

3 Prepare a list of the lawyers and doctors practising in your town or suburb. Are men and women equally represented? Do the sexes tend to do different sorts of work? Compare your findings with the information about those professional groups before World War II.

4 Visit the archives of your local newspaper. Do the earliest issues contain columns written for or by women? How do they compare to the 'gender balance' of the same paper today?

5 Visit your local hospital and speak with some of the nursing staff. Have conditions and expectations changed significantly since World War II?

6 Interview a female police constable at your local station. How do her duties differ from those of the men? Are they any different to what they would have been in Ruth Dunlop's day?

7   Women and the Arts

Max Meldrum, a painter and one of the most influential critics of Australian painting, remarked once that women and art were utterly incompatible. Eleanor Lucas would probably have agreed, although for different reasons. Burdened by the double responsibility of earning a living and raising a family, her paid and unpaid work left little time for artistic pursuits. The arts, Eleanor would probably have told us, were not for women like herself but for 'ladies'. In her lifetime at least, she was probably right. Most middle-class girls encountered the arts in the course of their education. The appropriate fee could buy a place in a school, salon or academy where the curriculum provided a solid grounding in the arts. And any self-respecting governess would give high priority to teaching her students what to read and how to write. The extension of education in the late nineteenth and early twentieth century did little to change this scenario. For all the public galleries, libraries and performances, the arts remained the luxury of those with money, time and education. (See Document 7.1.)

Achievement in the arts was an altogether different matter. Here women were restricted by their gender as well as their class. For all its pretensions to the unconventional, the world of the arts resisted change. Academies, conservatoriums and literary clubs were dominated by men, who were often uncomfortable with both the opposite sex and socio-economic groups other than their own. So while women might be permitted to paint at the academy, they were excluded from anatomy classes: the sight of a man's naked body, one director reasoned, was sure to provoke alarm. Others claimed 'biological weakness' prevented women from attempting large-scale portraiture. But the real reason for restricting women to landscapes was probably self-interest—portraiture paid well. Given that women's involvement in the arts was considered a hobby rather than a profession, it is not surprising that the most successful authors worked under male names—Ethel Richardson wrote as Henry Handel Richardson and

The getting of wisdom

The School year had ebbed; the ceremonies that attended its conclusion were over. A few days beforehand, the fifth-form boarders, under the tutelage of a couple of governesses, drove off early in the morning to the distant university. On the outward journey the candidates were thoughtful and subdued; but as they returned home, in the late afternoon, their spirits were not to be kept within seemly bounds. They laughed, sang, and rollicked about inside the wagonette, Miss Zielinski weakly protesting unheard—were so rowdy that the driver pushed his cigar-stump to the corner of his mouth, to be able to smile at ease, and flicked his old horse into a canter. For the public examination had proved as anticipated, child's play, compared with what the class had been through at Dr Pughson's hands; . . .

On the evening before the general dispersion, Laura, Cupid, and M.P. walked the well-known paths of the garden once again. While the two elder girls were more loquacious than their wont, Laura was quieter . . . glad as she felt to have done with learning, she was unclear what was to come next. The idea of life at home attracted her as little as ever—Mother had even begun to hint as well that she would now be expected to instruct her young brothers. Hence, her parting was effected with very mixed feelings; she did not know in the least where she really belonged, or under what conditions she would be happy; she was conscious only of a mild sorrow at having to take leave of the shelter of years.

Her two companions had no such doubts and regrets; for them the past was already dead and gone; their talk was all of the future, so soon to become the present. They forecast this, mapping it out for themselves with the iron belief in their power to do so, which is the hall-mark of youth.

Laura, walking at their side, listened to their words with the deepest interest, and with the reverence she had learned to extend to all opinions save her own.

M.P. proposed to return to Melbourne at the end of the vacation; for she was going on to Trinity, where she intended to take one degree after another. She hesitated only whether it was to be in medicine or arts.

'Oogh! . . . cut off people's legs!' ejaculated Laura. 'M.P., how awful.'

'Oh, one soon gets used to that, child—But I think, on the whole, I should prefer to take up teaching. Then I shall probably be able to have a school of my own some day.'

'I shouldn't wonder if you got Sandy's place here,' said Laura, who was assured that M.P.'s massy intellect would open all doors.

'Who knows?' answered Mary, and set her lips in a determined fashion of her own. 'Stranger things have happened.'

Cupid, less enamoured of continual discipline, intended to be a writer. 'My cousin says I've got the stuff in me. And he's a journalist and ought to know.'

'I should rather think he ought.'

'Well, I mean to have a shot at it.'

'And you, Laura?' M.P. asked suavely.

'Me?—Oh, goodness knows!'

'Close as usual, Infant.'

'No, really not, Cupid.'

'Well, you'll soon have to make up your mind to something now. You're nearly sixteen. Why not go on working for your B.A.?'

'No thanks! I've had enough of that here.' And Laura's thoughts waved their hands, as it were, to the receding figure of Oliver Cromwell.

'Be a teacher, then.'

'M.P.! I never want to hear a date or add up a column of figures again.'

'Laura!'

'It's the solemn truth. I'm fed up with all those blessed things.'

'Fancy not having a single wish!'

'Wish? . . . oh, I've tons of wishes. First I want to be with Evvy again. And then, I want to *see* things—yes, that most of all. Hundreds and thousands of things. People, and places, and what they eat, and how they dress, and China, and Japan . . . just tons.'

DOCUMENT 7.1 CONTINUED

'You'll have to hook a millionaire for that, my dear.'

'And perhaps you'll write a book about your travels for us stay-at-homes.'

'Gracious! I shouldn't know how to begin. But you'll send me all you write—all your books—won't you, Cupid? And, M.P., you'll let me come and see you get your degrees— every single one.'

With these and similar promises the three girls parted. They never met again. For a time they exchanged letters regularly, many-sheeted letters, full of familiar, personal detail. Then the detail ceased, the pages grew fewer in number, the time-gap longer. Letters in turn gave place to mere notes and post-cards, scribbled in violent haste, at wide intervals. And ultimately even these ceased; and the great silence of separation was unbroken. Nor were the promises redeemed: there came to Laura neither gifts of books nor calls to be present at academic robings. Within six months of leaving school, M.P. married and settled down in her native township; and thereafter she was forced to adjust the rate of her progress to the steps of halting little feet. Cupid went a-governessing, and spent the best years of her life in the obscurity of the bush.

And Laura? . . .

She went out from school with the uncomfortable sense of being a square peg, which fitted into none of the round holes of her world; the wisdom she had got, the experience she was richer by, had, in the process of equipping her for life, merely seemed to disclose her unfitness. She could not then know that, even for the squarest peg, the right hole may ultimately be found . . .

Stella Franklin as 'Miles'. Others wrote or exhibited anonymously, lest their work be judged as a woman's rather than a man's. More importantly, men like Meldrum decided what was 'art' and what was not. Traditionally women's most creative pursuits have had a practical purpose: letters and journals enabled one to keep in touch with friends and preserve a record of daily events; dressmaking and embroidery could be both useful and beautiful. But mediums such as these were frowned upon by a male-dominated arts establishment. Even today critics draw a clumsy distinction between 'art' and 'craft'. The natural history painter, Ellis Rowan, was exceptional in being able to defy the conventions of her day and carve out an international reputation from the denigrated female 'hobby' of flower painting.

(See Document 7.2.)

When women did excel in the arts it was usually on male terms. Dame Nellie Melba's phenomenally successful career in the opera was confined to a few female parts; for forty years she sang the stereotyped roles of wounded lover or unfaithful wife. Laurel Martyn danced the part of butterflies and maidens, her grace as a ballerina attributed to a woman's light touch.

Stereotypes such as these were subverted at a young artist's cost. In keeping with Australian convention, Miles Franklin and Katharine Susannah Prichard set their novels in the bush. Both faced the challenge of reinterpreting the bush in a way women might understand. While men celebrated mateship, Prichard discussed the meaning of sex. Franklin's female characters were

(Henry Handel Richardson, *The Getting of Wisdom* (1910), Heinemann Educational Books, Melbourne 1965, pp. 230–34. Reprinted by Permission of William Heinemann Limited.)

- When Cupid, M.P. (Mary) and Laura leave boarding school, what does each of them hope to be? How realistic do these expectations prove to be?

- Cupid thinks she's 'got the stuff in her' to be a writer. What do you think prevents her?

- Laura believes M.P.'s 'massy intellect will open all doors'—does it? What frustrates her aspirations? Is this a handicap for all ambitious women?

- Laura's mother has gone to a great deal of trouble and expense to secure her a good education. What does she see as Laura's future? Would she have hoped for the same for a son, rather than a daughter?

*According to Punch, writing
novels was a form of escape for both
reader and writer.*

(*Boomerang,* 28 March 1891)

THE SECRETS OF LITERARY COMPOSITION

The Fair Authoress of " Passionate Pauline," gazing fondly at her own reflection, writes as follows

" I look into the glass, Reader. What do I see?
" I see a pair of laughing, *espiègle,* forget-me-not blue eyes, saucy and defiant ; a *mutine* little rose-bud of a mouth, with its ever-mocking *moue* ; a tiny shell-like ear, trying to play hide-and-seek in a tangled maze of rebellious russet gold ; while from underneath the satin folds of a *rose-thé* dressing gown a dainty foot peeps coyly forth in its exquisitely-pointed gold morocco slipper, &c., &c.
(*Vide " Passionate Pauline," by Parbleu.*)

*Nellie Melba, 1900. Talent alone
was not enough. The right
connections and skilful promotions
'manufactured' Melba's success.*

(Promotion Australia)

'uppity', resourceful and independent, and could get by without men; Sybylla Melvyn in *My Brilliant Career* refuses an attractive offer of marriage to pursue her literary ideals. Both these writers were punished by their profession, their work proving far more popular in our day than their own. Definitions of what constitutes a good novel and, more importantly, what roles are suitable for women, have changed dramatically over time.

(See Document 7.3.)

Time and space are what all artists need to develop their work. Women often found both in short supply. For some the going was easier than others. Ethel (Henry Handel) Richardson was born into a comfortable middle-class family and married well. Her husband supported her work both financially and emotionally. He hired five servants to attend to her household and personally sharpened her pencils before departing each morning for work. And her domestic responsibilities were lightened in another way. The couple were childless; a necessary prerequisite if both were to excel in their careers. Nettie Palmer, by contrast, had the misfortune (so far as her career was concerned) to marry Vance. Her career took second place, and a promising young poet began her work as journalist and wife. Every day she hurried through her housework, carving out space in which to write.

DOCUMENT 7.2

My career goes bung

I had lots of other stuffing in me too. Resiliently I renewed my attack on LIFE. Rebellion against artificial WOMANLINESS did not interfere with all that rushed out of my mind on the wings of imagination. There was one great recreation open to me, even at 'Possum Gully', which was a sop to energy. I could ride. I could ride tremendously. I loved horses and seemed to become part of them. In the district were any number of good horses, most of them owned by bachelors. As one of these bachelors said, 'A lovely high-spirited girl is just the thing to top-off a good horse . . .'

Ma said that unless I meant to marry one of the men it was foolish and unladylike to be riding about with them; they would have no respect for me. If I really was against marriage I'd have to take up some trade or profession; she wished she had been trained to something so that she could be independent and not be dragged in the backwash of man's mismanagement.

This brought me to consider my prospects and to find that I hadn't any. I loved to learn things—anything, everything. To attend the University would have been heaven, but expense barred that. I could become a pupil-teacher, but I loathed the very name of this

profession. I should have had to do the same work as a man for less pay, and, in country schools, to throw in free of remuneration, the speciality of teaching all kinds of needlework. I could be a cook or a housemaid and slave all day under some nagging woman and be a social outcast. I could be a hospital nurse and do twice the work of a doctor for a fraction of his pay or social importance, or, seeing the tremendously advanced age, I could even be a doctor—a despised lady-doctor, doing the drudgery of the profession in the teeth of such prejudice that even the advanced, who fought for the entry of women into all professions, would in practice 'have more faith in a man doctor'. I could be a companion or governess to some woman appended to some man of property.

I rebelled against every one of these fates. I wanted to do something out of the ordinary groove. There were people who had done great things for the world, why not be one of such? Ma threw cold water on these haverings. Ma is the practical member of our ménage. She has to be, so that we have a ménage at all. Ma's thesis was that if all the millions who have gone have not improved the world, how was I going to do it in one slap? How would I start about it?

In a few minutes I'll knock off to get lunch ready . . . [Vance is] working now and I've just finished a sort of article between some bouts of housework . . . I want a bigger talent, and of course I want enough leisure to exploit the tiny talent I've got. Nothing short of jail could give me the leisure I'd need—a good stretch of solitary. Thank heavens Vance is working steadily and well.

Solitude never came. Nettie raised two daughters before resuming her broken career. Many of her contemporaries never married: writers like Miles Franklin, sculptors like Daphne Mayo, painters like Grace Cossington Smith, all found they worked better on their own. Others postponed marriage until late in life and remained childless. The sculptor Ola Cohn is an example. Margaret Preston, arguably the most important of Australia's women painters, married in her mid-forties, well after her reputation was made. And in Preston's case, marriage proved to

(Miles Franklin, My Career Goes Bung, Georgian House, Melbourne, 1946, pp. 20–21. Courtesy Collins/Angus & Robertson Publishers)

• Miles Franklin became one of Australia's greatest writers. But at a cost. What do these extracts tell us about her background and home life, what were the expectations of family and friends and what sort of sacrifice did she make in the pursuit of 'art'?

'One of the brainy old man-haters'

Henry Beauchamp was nearly a year away in Queensland. [When he returned] we reopened our old battles, he being armoured in the dogma that it was NATURE for women to serve men and bring children into the world regardless of whether or not the world was a fit place to receive them. He said he could give me much more than I could ever make by writing. 'Marriage,' he insisted, 'gives a woman standing. If she gets hold of a fellow with any sort of a head on him she has lots more standing than sour old school teachers and these other old maids, on their own, can have.'

STANDING!

'You don't allow a woman any standing at all except by being the annexation of a man,' I said.

He laughed in his large healthy way. 'Well, I did not arrange the world.'

'Yes, but you could help rearrange it,' I flashed, . . .

'Ah,' he continued complacently. 'You are not meant to be one of those brainy old man-haters who would rather have a snake around than a child. You were meant for love and motherhood.'

'Man-haters,' I contended, 'are those who are game enough to object to the present state of affairs for their motherhood. One such woman has more power of deep loving than half-a-dozen of the namby-pamby over-sexed womanised things.'

'Look here,' I warn Henry over and over again, 'don't you risk me in the matrimonial basket. Throw your handkerchief on one of the dozens of girls and widows who would snatch it eagerly. The world is infested with women who will agree with you—little darlings without intelligence, and boastful of it, who have been trained to be afraid of the night and to screech at a mouse and all that sort of thing.' . . .

'After your first child,' Henry maintained, 'you'll settle down as steady as a church.'

My first child! Something to break my spirit and tether me to the domestic tread-mill! Had he known my dreams of a first child he would not have uttered that mistake.

Even so, a first child need not last for ever. It could contribute to the fulfilment of life if it were not followed by a dozen others. I claim the same right as all the Father O'Tooles to be a spiritual parent of my race rather than . . . follow the example of . . . mother rabbit.

I repudiate the crawl theory that we should be servile to our parents or to God for the bare fact of a mean existence. Most people are satisfied with a world run in a wasteful insanitary fashion. I am not. They are unashamed that seventy-five per cent. of human beings are fit only for the scrap heap. I am not. They are thankful to thrive while others starve. I am not.

I rebel with all my lung force against sitting down under life as it is, and as for a first child being an instrument of enslavement, both for his own and his mother's sake, 'twere better he should never be.

The two greatest women in Australia are unmarried, and it would be a good plan for a few more to support them, to remain free to ventilate the state of marriage and motherhood and to reform its conditions.

'You just talk through your hat to be entertaining,' Henry continued after a while. 'You'll have to marry someone.'

'Why?'

'You could not endure to be despised as an old maid who could not get a man.'

At that I galloped right away from him leaving him a far speck on the glistening road that rises towards Lake George . . .

Despised for being an old maid, indeed! Why are men so disturbed by a woman who escapes their spoliation? Is her refusal to capitulate unendurable to masculine egotism, or is it a symptom of something more fundamental?

Why have men invented monogamy? All the laws, all the philosophies and religions of academic education, as well as organised fighting and politics, are men's inventions and are preserved by men as their special concern and business . . .

THOSE ELDERLY STAGE-BABIES.

THE DUCHESS OF FRANKFURTER: *Me chee-ild! me chee-ild! where can I find a hiding-place for you?*
STRIDENT VOICE FROM THE GALLERY: *Why don't you send her to boarding-school?*
—[*N.Y. Judge.*

Some actors started their careers at an early age but not soon enough, according to this cartoonist.

(*Boomerang*, 3 January 1890, p. 10

Art for some, agony for others—the Lone Hand (*a notoriously masculinist journal*) *could not resist satirising female opera singers.*

(*Lone Hand*, 1 August 1907)

be to the artist's advantage. Single she had taught to support herself; married she was supported by a man. Had Preston married earlier, the scenario would possibly have been very different. In all probability, Australia's most significant artist of the inter-war period would have put away her easel to raise children and keep house. Ellis Rowan's success was also partly attributable to family money and the fact that her relatives took over most of the care of her only son. Forsaking children and companionship was only one of the sacrifices these women made for their art. Many became expatriates, living, in Richardson and Christina Stead's case, most of their working lives away. On the one hand they were forced to do this because Australians undervalued their own artists. The belief that real culture, and real art, reside somewhere abroad has long been a part of Australia's cultural cringe. But their exile was also a comment on how male-dominated Australia has traditionally seen women.

Opposite: (Miles Franklin, *My Career Goes Bung*, Georgian House, Melbourne, 1946, pp. 224–9. Courtesy Collins/Angus & Robertson Publishers)

• Like many women writers, Miles Franklin was also a feminist. What does her quarrel with her lover Henry reveal about the 'inventions' and intentions of men?

The antique class at the Sydney Art Society. Often excluded from anatomy classes, female artists resorted to drawing from statues. To what social class do you think these women belonged?

(Reproduced in Robert Holden and Ingrid Holden, 'Women's Art and Craft Exhibitions in 19th Century Australia', *Hecate*, Vol. VI, No. 2, 1980, p. 119)

Margaret Preston, 'Self-Portrait', 1930.

(Estate of the late Margaret Preston. Art Gallery of NSW)

Notes

Nettie Palmer—Letter from Nettie Palmer to Frank Wilmot,
2 February 1928, Wilmot Papers, Mitchell Library, MS 4/7/111.
Cited in Dale Spender, *Writing a New World: Two Centuries of
Australian Women Writers*, London, Pandora, 1988, p.247.

SUGGESTIONS FOR STUDY

For discussion

1 Which of the arts do you think women have been most successful in? Why?

2 Virginia Woolf, an English writer, said that what women authors needed most urgently was one thousand pounds a year and 'a room of one's own'. What did she mean by this?

3 Is it any easier these days for Australian women to succeed in music, painting, acting, literature or dancing?

4 Does access to the arts still depend on one's class background?

5 The name of Henry Lawson is synonymous with Australian literature. Who was Louisa Lawson and what contribution did she make to the arts?

To write about

1 As we have seen, a number of Australia's most successful female writers (such as Miles Franklin, Henry Handel Richardson and Christina Stead) spent most of their adult lives overseas. Imagine that you were able to interview one of these authors. Write an article based on your interview, to be published in a literary magazine. Discuss the writer's reasons for becoming an expatriate.

2 You are the wife of a successful Brisbane lawyer, with some talent and enthusiasm for painting. Write a diary entry for one week in 1888, detailing the problems you experienced in pursuing this interest. You have three children under six years of age.

3 You are the child of a financially comfortable squatting family living in the Riverina. Mindful of the importance of 'female accomplishments', your mother has employed a governess who teaches piano and harp. What sacrifices must you make to pursue a concert career?

Community resources

Library, gallery and theatre

1 Consult any text on the arts in Australia. How much space is devoted to the artistic achievements of women as opposed to those of men? Of the women who were successful, how many were married with children of their own? Did successful men also have families?

2 Read one of Ruth Park's novels (*The Harp in the South, Poor Man's Orange*). Using the characters from the novels, draw up a series of case studies of women's working lives. Is Park's portrayal of the poor likely to be more sensitive than that of male authors? If so, in what respect?

3 Visit a local art gallery. How many women exhibit their work and how many men? Does their subject matter differ? Which is considered by critics to be 'better' art?

4 Look through the entertainment columns of any of the major daily papers. Which plays, ballets or operas performed by private or state companies were composed or written by women? How many of these women were Australian and how many are alive today? What does this say about the state of the arts in Australia?

8 Conclusion

Whether the women we have met in these pages were black or white, middle-class professionals or labourers, employed in big cities or provincial towns, married or single, young or old, they all had one thing in common—their working day did not end when they finished the day's paid work. Domestic chores of one kind or another waited on the attention of the wage-earning woman. And we have seen how this other world of unpaid work intruded on women's paid work, affecting their wages and influencing the kinds of jobs they could, or would, do. It is equally clear that the burdens of housework, bearing and caring for children and nursing the sick and elderly fell to Australia's women. Some could afford to pay for other women to help them in their homes, leaving them freer to take part in paid work and leisure. The amount of domestic labour required of any woman also varied according to the size, age, sex and health of her family and the extent to which other family members shared household tasks. The health and strength of the individual woman affected her ability to work 'double time', at both paid and unpaid work.

(See Document 8.1.)

The nature and experience of domestic work also varied with the passage of time. The years between the gold rushes of the 1850s and World War II saw the growth of Australia's major cities from small towns to sprawling metropolitan centres. The problems and tasks which confronted the colonial housekeeper and care-giver were often very different to those facing her counterpart in the 1920s or 1930s. In the days before sealed roads, electricity, gas, mains water, sewerage and detergents, cooking and cleaning were arduous and time-consuming. Such modern amenities made their appearance unevenly in Australia's cities and towns from the late 1880s to the 1930s, with the big cities leading the way. By the 1920s and 1930s even the houses of the working class had gas and electricity for heating, washing and lighting, and the sealed roads and sewerage networks had

DOCUMENT 8.1

Domestic happiness

PUBLIC NOTICES

" NEVER QUARREL

with a woman." We almost forget this saying when we hear of a housekeeper who hasn't sense enough to use

SAPOLIO.

A complete wreck of domestic happiness has often result-ed from badly washed dishes, from an unclean kitchen, or from trifles which seemed light as air. But by these things a man often judges of his wife's devotion to her family, and charges her with general neglect when he finds her care-less in these particulars. Many a home owes a large part of its thrifty neatness and its consequent happiness to SAPOLIO. No. 23.

(*Newcastle Herald*, 23 September 1890)

• What is this soap manufacturer selling besides soap? Is the image of marital relationships conveyed in the picture the same as that suggested by the accompanying text?

extended as far as city suburbs and provincial townships. At the same time, more affluent families were buying the new electric domestic appliances, such as washing machines, vacuum cleaners and floor polishers. All of these things made housework lighter and quicker.

There were other important changes to household work in these years. Families produced fewer things for their own use. Goods which had previously been made at home, such as soap, candles, clothes and preserved foods, were increasingly bought from a shop. Each purchase meant another time-consuming household chore eliminated.

(See Document 8.2.)

She's Getting a Man's Wages Now.

Not all men were happy with the prescribed roles for husbands and wives. This cartoon, pitched at a male market, conveys the resentment many men felt at the financial burdens imposed by marriage.

(*Smith's Weekly*, 9 April 1932)

DOCUMENT 8.2

Shopping in the 1890s

4350.   So far as you have noticed, are they the richer or the poorer class of people who buy their goods after 6 o'clock? — The poorer people, as a rule.

4351.   Do not you think they buy then because it is more convenient? — Some do, there is no doubt.

4352.   Do you think it is likely that there are any women with young children at home whom they are afraid to leave, and therefore they wait for their husband's return before going shopping? — Perhaps some do, but they need not.

4353.   How can a woman with a baby and young children manage? — The tradespeople call at their houses.

(Evidence of Mrs Agnes Milne, shirtmaker, Shops and Factories Royal Commission, South Australia, 1892, vol. 2)

• How have shopping patterns changed since the 1890s? How do these changes affect women's lives?

Another very important change in home life was the trend towards smaller families. From the 1860s middle-class couples had fewer and fewer children. By the 1920s and 1930s this was also true of working-class couples. Fewer children meant less housework, while fewer pregnancies reduced the physical costs of motherhood.

Did all these changes result in less unpaid work for women and more opportunities for paid work? Not necessarily. As housework became lighter, standards of housekeeping increased. The load might have been lighter, but it had to be carried more often. People washed themselves, their clothes and their homes more frequently. Sewing machines made dressmaking quicker, but women were expected to have more dresses. Gas and electricity made cooking quicker and less messy than open hearths or solid-fuel ranges, but meals were more elaborate and made much more washing-up. Fewer children did mean less housework for the family, but these children were more usually found at school rather than helping with child-care and chores. Mothers also lost the full-time help of their single daughters, as the twentieth century saw these young women leave the home each day for the shop, office or factory. On balance, the modernisation of housework freed single women for paid work, but for married women, especially mothers, housework itself remained a full-time job. And with the decline in personal domestic service between the wars, even middle-class women found themselves obliged to do much of this work themselves. Attitudes to women's work paralleled these developments. By the 1920s it was quite acceptable for single women of even the 'best' families to work outside the home. Attitudes to married women's paid work had, on the other hand, hardened. To be a working wife was to be not quite respectable.

(See Document 8.3.)

Wives who worked outside the home in the twentieth century were not only seen as not very respectable but also as a social menace. By doing paid work, it was argued, such women must necessarily be neglecting their duties in the home, especially the bearing and rearing of children. The quantity and quality of Australia's children was seen as vitally important to the country's

DOCUMENT 8.3   'In your home'

security in case of invasion. Many people argued that Australian women's first duty was to produce as many healthy children as possible. As if the burden of national security was not sufficient to deter mothers from doing paid work, they were also accused of taking jobs which rightly belonged to men or single women. Both these arguments were given added force by the experience of war from 1914 to 1918 and the onset of severe economic depression in 1929. By 1939, when war broke out in Europe again, the twentieth century had not brought freedom of choice or equal opportunities for Australia's working women. The sexual division of work had changed little in the previous eighty years. Women were still largely confined to a few 'female' occupations, to those jobs which had neither status nor adequate pay. The fact that men generally earnt so much more than women ensured that women continued to perform the bulk of domestic work, even had men been willing to exchange or share traditional roles. In this way the two spheres of work reinforced each other: woman's role as unpaid home worker limiting her opportunities in the job market, while low remuneration as an employee locked her into economic dependence on a male in exchange for unpaid domestic work. It was a vicious circle which few women in pre-World War II Australia had managed to escape.

(See Document 8.4.)

(*Australian Women's Weekly*, 9 January 1937)

(*Newspaper News*, September 1934. Mitchell Library, State Library of New South Wales)

• These advertisments from the 1930s are selling certain images of modern women along with their products. How are these images similar or different? If women accepted both the image and the products, do you think their domestic work would have been lightened?

DOCUMENT 8.4

The physical cost of a woman's work

Over-worked Women

The Suffering and Pain Endured by Many Women is Almost Beyond Relief.

THERE are thousands of Australian Women whose duties call them out in all weathers, often to sit with wet feet or stand all day, thus undermining their health. Many women, however, spend their lives at home, and these are ambitious that their homes should be kept neat and clean, their children well dressed and tidy, and they often do their own housework and sewing for the entire family. Truly, the work of such women "is never done," and is it any wonder that she breaks down at the end of a few years—the back aches, there is a general depression, and the struggle to continue her duties is pitiful? The reason is that the kidneys are not doing their duty. If they were, the blood would be kept pure and would nourish the whole body ; but, if the kidneys are inactive, the blood carries pain and disease throughout the system. Dr. Sheldon's Gin Pills are the great corrective for all Kidney ills, and in making the Kidneys well will soon remove such symptoms as Backache, Headache, Nervous Depression, Dragging Pains, Sleeplessness, Lassitude and other distressing ailments which women are so often subject to.

Diseased Kidneys and Gravel

"I have good cause to be grateful to Dr. Sheldon's Gin Pills," writes Mrs. M. Moore, The Avenue, Croydon, N.S.W. "I suffered from diseased kidneys and gravel for the past two years. I got so bad that I had to lay up for two weeks, my back was so painful. I could not sleep for the burning feeling all over me. To do my work was out of the question. I was really helpless. I tried numerous medicines, and wore a plaster for months, and I have been under two doctors ; but they all failed to give me any relief. One day I went to the chemist's to get something to give me a little relief, when I saw Dr. Sheldon's Gin Pills in the window. Being a new pill, I thought I would give them a trial. I bought a bottle, and after taking the contents I felt greatly relieved. They are far better than all the doctors and medicines put together. I took the pills for three months, and after that time I felt a new woman, and have not had a pain or an ache since."

For Backache and all Kidney Troubles use Dr. Sheldon's Gin Pills. One of those pills contains in a concentrated form all the curative properties of a pint of the finest gin, together with other important ingredients recognised by the medical profession as being remedial agents of the highest value for the kidneys and allied organs.

Dr. Sheldon's Gin Pills are procurable at all chemists and storekeepers in two size glass containers. Small size at *1/6*, large size at *2/6*, or six bottles of the large size for *13/6*. Or, if not obtainable locally, will be sent post free upon receipt of price in stamps or postal note by Sheldon Drug Co., Ltd., 15 O'Connell Street, Sydney, N.S.W.

Dr. Sheldon's GIN PILLS
FOR BACKACHE AND KIDNEY TROUBLES.

(*Lone Hand*, 2 October 1911)

• What does this advertisement suggest about the nature of women's working lives? What sort of women does it appeal to—rural or urban, young or old, single or married? Why would women be likely to resort to Dr Sheldon's Gin Pills? What remedy would 'overworked women' seek today?